TENNIS CIRCUITRY:

MASTER THE SOFTWARE
OF A PROFESSIONAL TENNIS PLAYER

JASON GOLDMAN-PETRI

CONTENTS

SOFTWARE:

The internal programs and other operating
information used to run the system (YOU!)

SECTION 1:

REHEARSAL

A practice or trial performance of a play
or other work for later public performance.

CHAPTER 1

EVALUATION

The first step in every good endeavor is a proper evaluation. When there is something wrong with your computer, you run diagnostics, so just think of this evaluation as running diagnostics on your tennis.

Now imagine you have a brand-new computer with brand-new software, but someone infected it with a virus. Even though everything is up to date, nothing is going to seem right. After a year you might decide to upgrade the software, or replace a piece or two of hardware, but no matter what you try, everything is going to move a little slower, be a little sluggish, or just seem off. That is what having bad practice routines amounts to: A VIRUS.

Proper practice is so important because tennis is a skill-based sport. When it comes to skill building, it is easy to accidentally slow down the process. I took Spanish in school from the 2nd grade all the way up until 10th grade, and while I *can* say, "Como está?" I am also INCREDIBLY unskilled. There are people who learn Spanish fluently in as little as a year, so why do I still suck after nine years of learning the language? I probably did a whole lot of things wrong. (Lo siento, Señor Pepe.)

When it comes to tennis, we are on an incredibly unfair timeline. We must learn so many skills: serve, forehand, backhand, volley, etc. Yet we have so little time to do it to realize a career as a professional because we can only keep running down shots for so long before our bodies catch up with us.

> ## Anything that slows down the process needs to be nixed ASAP.

Two important aspects of skill building that you will need to remember...

#1: Bad habits are not a crutch, so stop using them as one

Let's say you are doing something wrong with your forehand that you have been doing incorrectly for *years*. You do not have to UNDO the years of incorrect practice. However, you will have to build the new aspect of your forehand up to the same level that the old forehand was, *and you will be starting from **nothing***. At first you will suck but changing will be worth it if you're learning the correct technique. If you think that it is not worth changing something that is potentially limiting you simply because it is a well ingrained bad habit, you are seriously underestimating the power of correct skill building.

A car going down a dirt road. If you go down the ruts where previous wheels have gone, it will be difficult to get out. Skill building is not like that; instead, you will be starting a new rut where no wheels have gone. The new ruts will not yet be deep because they will need to be repeated many times first.

#2. You do not learn from your mistakes (in a skill-building sense)

When researchers hooked people's brains up to scanners and had them do skill building activities, they found something very interesting. People did not imprint new skills when they did the task incorrectly (in tennis terms, hitting it OUT), but only when they were successful (hitting it IN). We do not learn from our mistakes in the sense that we learn the skill. Instead, we gain only limited guidance about how to do subsequent attempts correctly. This means we need to hit at speeds we can control and drill skills until we are good at them before trying those techniques in a match. To form habits and learn skills, we need to be doing them correctly, and we need to be doing them A LOT!

> The adage that we learn from our mistakes does *not* apply to tennis; we learn when we are successful.

How do I know if I am practicing correctly or not?

Ask yourself these questions to determine if there is a potential issue with the way you practice:

Do you practice in a controlled environment so that you are having success?

If not, you need some drills that slow things down for you and give you a chance to focus on what you are practicing.

Is your practice repetitive enough?

Repetition creates habits and helps solidify the skill quickly.

Are you practicing something that will lead to performance enhancements in your next tournament?

Are you sure what you are practicing is the correct thing to be practicing?

If you trust your coach knows what they are doing, listen to them, even if they say put a target on your head.

This is what the rest of the book is about (this book's complement is about the hardware of tennis, which includes things like your physical training and technical training).

For now, just ask yourself, "Do you trust that your coach knows what they are talking about and is sending you down a path towards greatness?" If so, then freakin' listen to their advice already! If not, then read this book carefully and find someone else who is more in tune with the messages throughout this book. After all, you can't achieve greatness all on your own.

No matter what you decide to change about your game, no matter whether it is a technical skill, a tactical element, a physical component, or a mental/ emotional intelligence, you will need a good practice regimen to see that change through to fruition.

How does this all work?

Let's say I have a new student and I want to evaluate their practice rehearsal and determine whether the way they are making changes is as good as it could be. The first thing I will ask the student is what skills they are working on. It is incredibly important that students set goals for themselves, and not just year to year or month to month. I would want to hear from the student what the goal of that exact exercise is. If students are not aware of why it is exactly that they are doing what they are doing, then we already have a BIG problem.

Next what I would ask what stage they are in. This is a tricky question because we haven't talked about periodization yet (that's the next part), but basically what I want to know is how long they have been working on that specific element. This is very important to understanding what drills we should use, what the intensity level should be, and where their focus should be. If the student is working on something for the very first time, I would expect their drills to be very slow and controlled. If the student has been working on this area for a week or two, I would expect their drills to be more live ball with some tactical elements included. And finally, if they have been working on something for a month, I would want to see that they can execute it in a realistic situation and are preparing to test its effectiveness in a tournament.

Proper goal setting helps to keep things on track.

Some ways I have seen people mess this up:

If you are working on something new every day you won't ever develop the skill to the point where it can be executed well in a tournament situation. Over time, your training needs to shift away from fed ball drills to more live ball and

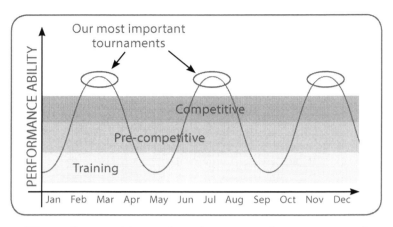

We can't expect to work on key areas of our game and maintain a high level of playing ability at all times, so we must plan accordingly.

match play situations. Finally, if you are like most people, you may practice once or twice during the week and then play a practice match on the weekends or after training. This is a bad idea if you want to learn a new skill because you just put yourself in a situation where you will not realistically be successful. You won't be learning, and you probably inadvertently sabotaged your training because you will want to revert to old habits, so you can win. When that happens, it is like starting over. This can mean that it takes much longer to effectively learn new skills and improve at a quick enough rate to make it as a pro.

This is the most important part of the book and why I started with it. If you do not have all the proper elements of a good practice rehearsal in place it won't matter what you do; you will always be stunted. No expert coach, no amount of effort, and no innate talent can overcome such a huge obstacle.

CHAPTER 2

PERIODIZATION

Periodization is the proper planning of practice to maximize performance for key moments. The key moments should come in periodic waves so that in between there is time for evaluation and training. This is a way for the brain to learn and improve for the next performance. In tennis, we have the luxury of planning our own tournament schedule. If we do things right, we can map it out so that we are performing at our best for the most important events.

Training block

The first element you need in the periodization calendar is the training block. This is something most people mess up. The training block is a time where coach and player are walled off. There should be **NO** match play, and *a lot* of one on one time with the coach. The coach is the teacher and the player is the student. The training block can be as little as a week to as much as a month, depending on how difficult the change is. Younger players will have longer training blocks as they are typically making more major changes, and they will need more of them throughout the year as they have more to learn.

If you want to make major changes to your game, you are not going to be able to do it in just one week. You will need to plan accordingly. You can, of course, make multiple changes to your game during a training block, but it is not good practice to try and make multiple changes to the same *element*. As an example, trying to change your forehand backswing and the follow through of the forehand at the same time would be too much about the swing. In contrast, trying to change your stance and your backswing would be OK, because one is a footwork element and the other is a swing element.

Coach and Player working on technique in a controlled environment.

Step #1: Evaluate

A good training block begins with an evaluation (which is different from an evaluation of whether you are practicing correctly). This evaluation is to determine what needs you have as a player. With that knowledge you can come up with a plan to tackle those needs.

As an example, let's say in the past tournament you were outgunned by your opponent's offense to your backhand side. That tells me you need to work on your defensive backhand skills.

In your periodization you need to determine the best course of action for fixing this problem. Are you going to work on footwork so that you can set up to hit better defense? Are you going to work on shortening your backswing so that you can make contact out in front when the ball comes faster or is hit deeper? Are you going to work on upper body strength, so you can absorb that power better and redirect even if you make contact late? Are you going to incorporate a slice more often?

These are all possible scenarios that could help your defensive backhand and you can't expect yourself to do all these things at the same time. This is one reason you need a trained coach who can help you identify what area will garner the biggest reward. Together you can figure out how best to improve that aspect in the upcoming training block.

Step #2: Isolate

Now that you know what you are planning to work on, you need to set up some drills to isolate that area. Let's stay with the backhand example and decide to work on a slice backhand. Let's also say you've never concentrated on this shot before.

Get in close to the net and hit a few slow balls first to get a feel for it. Then slowly back up and start picking up your pace more and more while the coach explains how to do it correctly. After a week or so of drills, you will probably be able to move on to some live ball hitting where you can also begin to mix it up between topspin and slice. Remember, this improvement in the backhand is not the only change you will make, so it will not be the only drill that you do, but it will be the only drill you do that will pertain to the defense on the backhand.

Coach and Player working on technique in a controlled environment.

Step #3: Incorporate

The reason you want this slice in your arsenal is to help you in your next match. It is sometimes hard for tennis coaches and players to remember that these skills do not exist in a bubble. They serve a function, and in this case, the function is to play better defense. There needs to be a tactical component to the skill that is worked into the end of a training block.

In this case, we want to incorporate some knowledge about WHEN we should slice versus when it might be a better idea to stick to our topspin. We also want to think about how the slice might tactically set up our ability to slowly turn defense back into offense. Without the tactical component linked with the skill, we are just working on the skill in a bubble and with no purpose. Combining the skill with purpose is what guarantees it will help us get the results we are seeking.

Slicing when wide of the court is an essential defensive tactic.

Pre-competitive block

Now that you are confident about your slice and your ability to hit it in a controlled environment, you are ready to move into the pre-competitive block. A pre-competitive block can be as little as a week, but usually shouldn't be more than two weeks. A pre-competitive block is designed to prepare you for a competition. If you are preparing and preparing and never competing, you will never know how well your skill will hold up under pressure or if you missed something crucial to learning it. At the same time, if you skip the pre-competitive block before you start competing, you most likely will not perform well either.

The goal for a good pre-competitive block is to introduce some control elements to the changes being made and work on ways to seamlessly weave them into the way the player competes. With the slice backhand, that may require that you keep it low or deep and understand how those different control elements affect the opponent. It may also mean increasing your tactical understanding of the skill, or it may just mean making sure the skill is competition ready.

> **You learned how to DO the skill, now you need to learn how to USE the skill.**

That means that the pre-competitive block needs to closely mimic competition. This could be game based, where you feed it to the backhand forcing the slice and then play it out. Or it could be more like real points, having the coach

Learning how to use a new skill requires different drills than learning how to do it. Coach isn't the teacher; now they are more of a coach.

watching closely and giving feedback about where good decisions were made and where things still need adjustment. In a pre-competitive block, if things break down or your confidence begins to wane, there can be a little bit of drilling as well, but mostly the block is about utilizing the new skill in a more open environment (open meaning more variables and/or more realistic practice).

> ## Drilling endlessly is not the quickest way to improvement.

You may believe that a coach should always be drilling, or that a player should always be working on things, constantly making changes. However, it is best to single out the most important thing and try to ignore everything else. This will allow you to tackle that error and refine it to a habit more quickly. You are not going to be able to fix everything in a short amount of time, but certainly if you focus on one small aspect, drill it in the training block, and then learn how to use it effectively in the pre-competitive block, you can reasonably expect that it will improve enough to see an increase in performance for the next tournament.

Can you do this *and* be aware that other issues exist? OF COURSE! But if you try to tackle too many changes all at once you doom yourself to an excruciatingly long learning process or worse, never actually learning the skill. You will not have enough processing power to divert your attention that many ways. That is why I suggest strategically ignoring areas that are not currently your focus until these issues have been tackled.

Since we can't fix everything, we need to make sure we are targeting the most important changes.

Competitive block

This all leads very nicely to the last stage of the periodization, the competitive block, where you will be competing. Sometimes you will just have one tournament in the competitive block, but in higher levels of competitive tennis you may end up with many more tournaments. As an example of how this all plays out, when the pros are gearing up for the Australian open, they normally have not played a tournament since the end of November, and they have an entire month in December to rest before beginning a training block. After training, they may do some warm-up exhibitions or small tournaments (pre-competitive block) before the Australian open.

They only have one or two tournaments max before they play the Australian open (two- or three-tournament competitive block) and then almost everyone returns to another training block. This nice set-up often leads to a very high quality of play at the Australian open because the tournament schedule more closely aligns for good periodization planning.

How much competition is the right amount?

In stark contrast, the road to Roland-Garros has many more tournaments of high importance that lead to the big finale at the French Open. It can be tricky for the best players in the world to manage their periodization, as too much competition can make a player feel drained mentally and physically, whereas not enough tournament preparation may hurt their performance as well. Rafael Nadal likes to play many, many warm-up tournaments, while Roger Federer prefers a few. You will need to know what works best for you and plan accordingly. You won't know what works best for you right away, but you probably already have a sense of which you prefer. For instance, if I play too many tournaments back to back, I start to get very tight and lose my natural flow. When I return to training, I regain the right feeling. Other players get nervous if they haven't played a tournament in a while; they need a warm-up tournament to get back into the competitive mindset.

Most people mess up the competitive block in one of two ways:

- Some people incorrectly believe they should compete every single week and they end up never getting a chance to perfect their technique in a controlled environment.

- Other people will play a tournament, not do well, and then instead of learning from their mistakes in the tournament and going back to a new training block with new areas to work on, they just add on another tournament.

Obviously we want to do well in our tournaments, and we do need to play a certain number in order to maintain our ranking, but the real benefit of the periodization is that it is set up in a way that gets players to peak performance for the most important tournaments (this unfortunately doesn't *guarantee* a win, but it certainly is better than no planning). Another tournament may seem like a good idea, but there is no benefit to over-competing. It robs you of the chance to get back to a training block which is where real improvements occur.

How to plan out your own periodization

Now that you have read all about periodization, it is time to set one up for yourself. The easiest way to set up a periodization plan is to look ahead at your tournament schedule and figure out which ones you want to prepare for. Let's pretend we are preparing for a grand slam, and if we are going to prepare for a grand slam, shouldn't we prepare for the most grandiose of slams? We're going after the *crème de la crème*, the coup de grace, the biggest stage in tennis, the US FREAKIN' OPEN! OK, I may just be a little too 'Murican, but let's say this is a big deal to you. *You are going to want to play your best.*

Perhaps you are the type of player who wants to go in fresh to the US Open and only play two or three warm-up events. You have a choice of playing the Citi Open, then the Rogers Masters, then Western & Southern, and then Winston-Salem before the US open.

Which tournaments do you play?

This is where it gets tough, and where a lot of players would shoot themselves in the foot. If you decide to play three warm-up events, the first one would be the Rogers Masters. That tournament is a really big deal. You will want to do well in that tournament and so you ought to add on another warm-up tournament at the Citi Open. But now you have four tournaments before the US Open and you prefer only two or maybe three. If you want to win the US FREAKIN' OPEN, you had better plan the lead up very intelligently. You may just have to skip—*gasp*—the Rogers Masters—*gasp*—.

"Is this dumb-dumb for real?" you are probably asking yourself. "No pro skips the Rogers Masters!" (BTW, the Master of Planning, Roger Federer, just skipped the Rogers Masters, so clearly, I am not THAT crazy.) Over-competing is probably why many players are burnt out by the time they get to the US Open, because the US Open lead up is incredibly long and grueling. My bet is when you see the two periodization calendars mapped out you will start to understand why proper planning is so important.

If you play the five warm-up tournaments, with a pre-competitive block AND training block, then you will be devoting your entire summer to preparing for the US Open with no real place for rest. It's even worse if you compete at Wimbledon in July. Now your training block is just a week-long process where you barely have time to make any meaningful changes. You will probably be tired from Wimbledon because right before Wimbledon is the French Open and there is zero time between those two events. WOW! Good luck doing anything significant at the US Open with a schedule like that.

Here are the two calendars fully mapped so you can see the difference:

- Wimbledon July 1-14
- Start training block July 15
- Start pre-competitive block July 22
- Citi Open July 29-August 4
- Rogers Masters August 5-11
- Western & Southern August 11-18
- Winston-Salem August 18-25
- US Open August 26-September 8

With this schedule, you have no rest unless you lose early in Wimbledon, but then no room for breaks as you will be playing, training, or competing every week right up until the US Open. You had better not have any injuries or need to work on anything if you want to play well at the US Open.

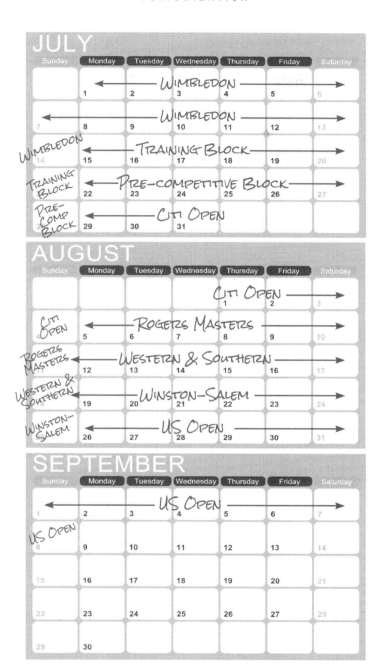

JULY

Sunday	Monday	Tuesday	Wednesday	Thursday	Friday	Saturday
	1 ←	2 *WIMBLEDON*	3	4	5 →	6
7 ←	8	9 *WIMBLEDON*	10	11	12 →	13
14 *WIMBLEDON*	15 ←	16 *TRAINING BLOCK*	17	18	19 →	20
21 *TRAINING BLOCK*	22 ←	23 *PRE-COMPETITIVE BLOCK*	24	25	26 →	27
28 *PRE-COMP BLOCK*	29 ←	30 *CITI OPEN*	31			

AUGUST

Sunday	Monday	Tuesday	Wednesday	Thursday	Friday	Saturday
				1 *CITI OPEN*	2 →	3
4 *CITI OPEN*	5 ←	6 *ROGERS MASTERS*	7	8	9 →	10
11 *ROGERS MASTERS* ←	12	13 *WESTERN & SOUTHERN*	14	15	16 →	17
18 *WESTERN & SOUTHERN*	19 ←	20 *WINSTON-SALEM*	21	22	23 →	24
25 *WINSTON-SALEM*	26 ←	27 *US OPEN*	28	29	30 →	31

SEPTEMBER

Sunday	Monday	Tuesday	Wednesday	Thursday	Friday	Saturday
1 ←	2	3 *US OPEN*	4	5	6 →	7
8 *US OPEN*	9	10	11	12	13	14
15	16	17	18	19	20	21
22	23	24	25	26	27	28
29	30					

This is a better alternative:

- Wimbledon July 1-14
- Week of rest (well-earned rest after having done warm up tournaments for the French open, playing the French, then starting warm up tournaments for Wimbledon and then playing Wimbledon)
- Start training block July 22th
- Start pre-competitive block Aug 5th (that's two whole weeks of training after having rested, so it might be good training and not just going through the motions)
- Western & Southern
- Winston-Salem
- Finally, the US Open

Of course, there are other ways to do this. Many players who feel they have a real shot at winning will take off the Winston-Salem tournament, so they can rest their bodies. They know if they play the Rogers AND a warm-up tournament, they will be exhausted going into the US Open. But what about those people who want to just do better at the US Open? Perhaps they normally lose in the first round and they want to make it to the third round. That type of a player would benefit from proper planning. They would have a better shot at improving their performance by taking the time to seriously train instead of constantly competing and burning themselves out.

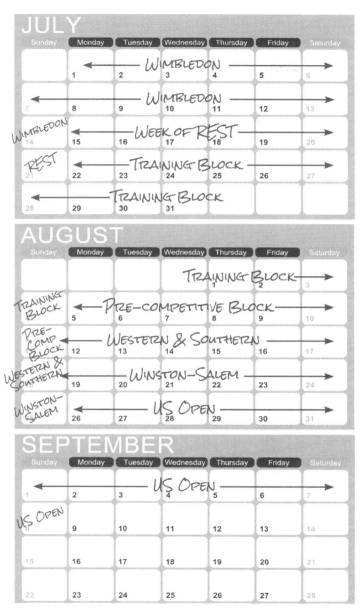

Planning out your calendar will give you the clearest path to greatness possible.

What should be included in a good periodization?

When I do a proper periodization, I include a lot of information in the plan and have numerous things to consider depending on the client. My periodization will include the goals of the player, both for the year and for the training period, as well as a written understanding of how this planning will lead to successful completion of their larger dream goals. I include information about each week's focus and things like drill selection. If the player is in a pre-competitive block, I will indicate what level of player they are ideally practicing against. I include fitness, mental, tactical, and technical elements to work on during the training period. I also include days of rest each week and if possible, a large rest (3-5 days minimum) after the whole period has completed.

Goal setting is an important part of the periodization planning process.

How often do you think my clients and I end up sticking to a periodization perfectly?

Ha ha, never. Not even once. I've come close a few times though!

That is because a plan is not reality, and it certainly should not be adhered to dogmatically. There are so many things that will disrupt the flow of the plan and you will inevitably have to adjust. That is just fine. Understand the purpose of the plan; it gives clarity and purpose to your training and can be used to decide which adjustments need to be made.

What happens if you miss a day because of rain? Do you pick things back up the next day or do you make it a day of rest?

If you look at your calendar and see that an extra day of rest won't affect your ability to prepare, you may want to keep it that way. But if you are only one week into training, you will have more days of rest later. Now you are doing things at a low intensity because you have just started learning a new element. You can easily get back to work the next day and not be physically or mentally tired. In that case, there's no need for a day of rest. Without a proper periodization plan, you would have been just taking a stab in the dark. With it, you can make an informed decision.

Here is what I would do if I were you:

First, I would look at the tournament schedule and decide which major event to compete in. Don't look too much farther than six months ahead because any planning beyond that becomes too convoluted. Then plan backwards based on your tournament schedule. Figure out which warm-up tournaments might be needed, if any. I don't recommend scheduling too many tournaments back-to-back until you reach very high levels, as playing a lot of tournaments without rest is typically where symptoms of burnout creep in. Then count back at least one week from the warm-up tournament and designate that as your pre-competitive block. For this time block, you will need to find hitting partners for match play and live ball drills. A coach can do this if you don't have players readily available, but that is never going to be as realistic as a peer. The last step is to determine how much training you will need. Think about which areas were difficult for you in your previous tournament. Consult with your coach, and perhaps even your physiotherapist and talk about what you need to improve. Think about how long it will realistically take to learn that aspect. The younger the player, the more technical work is required, so if you are younger give yourself longer training blocks as you will have a harder time implementing big technical changes.

> I know what some of you are thinking, do I *have to* do this to be professional? Can't I just think of this in my head because this seems like a lot of work?

Can you run a business without quarterly goals and a marketing plan to help achieve those goals? Sure, but if you are always guessing where you are and never take time to plan, you will not do as well as those who are more organized. If everyone is driven, everyone is working hard, and everyone has good people around them, how will you separate yourself from the pack? A proper plan is exactly the type of thing coaches and players neglect and that is exactly why you should take the time to be organized in this way.

The vast majority of players are just winging it. That's why so many feel they haven't lived up to their potential.

CHAPTER 3

REPETITION

> Repetition: The recurrence of an event...
> a training exercise that is repeated.

Tennis is a highly repetitive game. We are tasked with hitting roughly a hundred serves, tons more forehands and backhands, and running the same tactical patterns match in and match out without much room for experimentation or creative flair. In my eyes the hardest part in all of this is that there are certain shots that we do not hit very often. What happens when I am playing my match and I am confronted with a lob over my backhand side that I need to hit inside out to avoid going straight back to my opponent?! That's a freakin' crazy scenario because no one gets to hit that shot often enough just from playing matches to have it nailed down. What that means is that in practice we must hit it enough times to not only hit it well, but also be confident enough in our ability to not lose focus or accidentally get tight.

> Then my question is, how many
> repetitions will that take?

Growing up, my coach had a funny way of describing this. He would say things like, "Jason, why do I make you hit ten in a row when you will never have to hit that many in a match during one point?" His answer was...

"RTB"

RTB stands for *Reason To Believe*. To be confident in a shot we need a *reason to believe* that when push comes to shove, we're going to make the shot. RTB requires tons and tons of repetitions, and more so than that, correct repetitions that go _IN_!

> Remember from earlier that we do not
> learn skills when we miss.

What we are defining is the difference between missing the easy ball versus putting it away, the difference between being able to concentrate under pressure versus choking, and the difference between winning versus losing. The difference is the thousands of correct repetitions that allow us to feel confident in a shot. No matter the situation, we need to feel like we have a *REASON TO BELIEVE* we can do it.

Correct Repetition

Anders Ericsson did a lot of the science experiments that allow us to know so much about skill-building. Anders played chess his whole life but didn't understand why he didn't play as well as his opponents. Instead of being normal and just drinking his problems away (which is what most people would have done) Anders went on to study the best chess players in the world to see how they practiced to become world-class. What he found was that they practiced differently from most. Instead of just playing a game of chess or two they would scrutinize one move over and over for hours. Most of that time was spent finding every possible counter-move and every intricacy of a certain decision. Even though this type of practice was not always fun, and was highly repetitive and time consuming, it gave those players an edge should that one move ever occur again. (In case you were wondering, when Anders started practicing correctly, he became amazing at chess).

These critical studies led Anders to discover the concepts of deliberate practice. That forms our understanding of a correct repetition.

You will need to repeat specialized shots enough to have confidence in them under pressure

The learning phase

Now that you have a little scientific background about skill building, it's time to put that into tennis-specific ideas. You heard me say, "correct repetitions." That is going to be super-important to how we practice.

"What is a correct repetition?"

I am glad you asked:

> A correct repetition is when you are focused on just one small aspect of a skill, whether it is a technical or tactical element, or a footwork or physical element.

If you are in the learning phase you won't know if you did it correctly. In this case, you need a coach or some other form of feedback like video analysis to help you determine if you did it correctly. It will be very important in this early stage to control the learning environment, because if things are too difficult you will not be able to do the new skill AND get it IN.

> **After all, it's hard to believe in something that never goes IN the court.**

Here is an example of what a correct repetition would look like in the learning phase:

Let's say you are working on staying balanced on your serve after you hit. Your coach might tell you that he wants you to land on your front foot and hold that position after hitting instead of getting ready to hit the next shot to demonstrate good balance in the landing phase. If you push off and hit, land on your front leg, and then immediately must put your other foot on the ground, your coach will tell you that you were not balanced. That is not a correct repetition, even if the ball went in and you did in fact land on your front leg. To make it a correct repetition, you would need to exaggerate the balance point and hold the landing long enough to feel like you could stand there without falling over. If you teeter or fall, then you are not balanced. If you end up being balanced but miss the shot, then you should try serving slower or from closer in to give yourself a chance to be successful in the drill.

Based on that example, I can already tell where a big problem might come into play. Many players will only tell themselves that it was a correct repetition if the ball goes in, regardless of whether they did it correctly. However, if you are making a meaningful change that will help your performance, it may be too difficult at first to get the ball in as consistently as you want and THAT IS FINE! You should still try to get it in (and will possibly have to dial down the difficulty level as we talked about), but you will have plenty of chances to get the ball in at full speed once you have progressed out of the *learning phase* and into the *acquisition phase*.

Details such as being balanced are crucial in the learning phase.

Acquisition phase

We then move on to what a correct repetition is in the acquisition phase. In the acquisition phase, you will need to make the correction to your game in more and more difficult scenarios and at closer to game-like conditions. As you progress you need to make sure that first and foremost you are focusing on the change and that you are adding in difficulty slowly. When you have gone through the most difficult scenarios where you can still do it correctly, only then should you worry about whether it will hold up in a match. Your belief grows with each level you overcome and with each shot that you make with the improved skill. You won't have much to believe in if you try to move on too quickly or immediately start playing matches. Those players who try to move along too quickly without taking these proper steps often end up reverting to old habits under the pressure of a match.

Here is what a correct repetition would look like in the acquisition phase:

Going back to the example of the serve, eventually you will expand off that initial balanced landing position. It is one thing to be able to land balanced off *one* type of serve, but good servers must do that off their flat, slice, top, and kick serves. NOT ONLY THAT, you will also need to land balanced, and then immediately recover and hit the next shot. This is where the balanced landing position starts to integrate into a meaningful tactical understanding of the game. It serves a purpose now and so the drills, situations, and understanding of the skill change. You will obviously need to have different repetitions for the different spins, and different repetitions for whether you are recovering for a hard-hit return or a weak one that you can attack. You will still be thinking diligently about the change, and you will still be drilling, but it will now include a more competitive experience to integrate the skill into a meaningful game plan.

These skills must function in a real environment, so we must constantly increase the difficulty.

Mastery phase

Finally, as we enter in the mastery phase, our definition of a correct repetition will change one final time. In the mastery stage, you no longer need to be put into a controlled environment. You have no more "learning" to do in the traditional sense of the word, but you still will have months or even years left to go before you can perform the skill subconsciously without any thought whatsoever. You still need to be doing a little bit of thinking, maintaining an awareness of change, and giving yourself a sliding scale for evaluating its correctness. So instead of it being a black and white, "yes, correct" or "no, incorrect," it will be more like, "Was I balanced on that serve? Why or why not? How accurate was it? I missed that serve but it felt good and I was balanced, so I am OK with that one."

Good-miss, bad-make

This last phase is weird because we will be tasked with executing changes in real game situations and with far more pressure than in any drill. For the mastery phase, I like to introduce the concepts of a *good-miss* and a *bad-make*. If you want to make changes quickly and effectively you will need to give yourself an extra cushion. If you do the correction correctly under pressure in a real situation but you happen to miss it, you should give yourself a little encouragement and say, "That's OK, it was a good-miss," (good because you did the new skill correctly). On the other hand, if you fold to the pressure and forget to do your changes or you are so worried about making a mistake that you allow yourself to revert to an old habit, you should stop yourself and catch it before all your hard work from training eludes you. This is when you should tell yourself, "I don't care if that shot went IN. It wasn't correct, and therefore it was a bad-make." (You made the shot which is normally good but because you didn't do the new skill you are not getting better and therefore it was bad.)

Here is an example of a good-miss bad-make mentality in the mastery phase of skill building:

Using our example of the balanced position for the service landing phase one last time, we now move into full-on highly competitive situations where the pressure is "on like Donkey Kong." You no longer have the luxury of a controlled environment as your opponent will be trying to pummel you. You hit a second serve and you do not bounce back to hit the return quickly enough. You now should ask yourself WHY you didn't bounce back quickly enough. If it was because you were not balanced when landing after the serve, then you have just committed a bad-make. Sure, the ball went in on the serve, but because you were not balanced, you couldn't bounce back to hit a decent defensive shot. Next time you step up to the line, make sure you land balanced on that second serve. Will you double fault? Sure, it is possible. But

Sometimes we do not hit our target but that is OK in the mastery phase as long as we are sticking to our changes.

if you do, you can look back and say, "Well, I am pretty sure I was at least balanced on that one." Then you have just had a good-miss.

> This should be easy,
> yet it is SO SO HARD!

If you combine correct repetitions with proper periodization you will get a clear idea of how to make the most of your practices. You are probably seeing how you may have screwed this up before. You only have two or so weeks of training before you are in a pre-competitive phase. If you are working on a technique, plan to isolate it to just ONE change and try not to do too much at once. The problem with trying to tackle too many changes is that you only have so much mental processing power. As soon as you start inputting more and more stress from the reality of the game, you are going to inevitably throw something away to be successful. Or, just as bad, you end up working on a lot but not actually perfecting any one thing. Here you end up with a bunch of changes that you can't fully execute when it comes time to compete.

This is a costly mistake and is ultimately what makes players revert to old habits under pressure. You didn't give yourself the opportunity for enough correct repetitions because you had too much to work on and so now you have no real *reason to believe* it will work. Confronted with the prospect of losing and keeping your changes or discarding them and winning, most athletes will just drop the changes and try to win. After all, you wouldn't really be a good competitor if you didn't want to win, now would you?

> You wanted these changes because of their potential to make you better. By not practicing correctly you end up sacrificing long term gains for winning in the short term.

If you do not practice correctly, it means you are doomed to repeat the learning process over again. This will slow you down and hold you back *just that little bit*. Do it enough times and you will see how players end up never achieving their potential and see a promising pro career slip away.

Implementation time

Map out your own periodization and practice schedule.

Here's a typical 14 and under periodization:

- 2-week training block
- 1-week pre-competitive block
- 1-week competitive block
- Repeated 10 times for approx. 12-14 tournaments a year with 2 months of vacation throughout the year (Christmas/New Year's), Thanksgiving, spring break, end of summer, etc.

Example:

Day 1—figure out what areas need improvement based on your performance in the last tournament. Test to set a benchmark to determine if the changes you make are effective (could be physical testing, like how fast can you move side to side 10 times, or skill testing, like how many forehands can you make in a row, etc).

Goals for this period include:

- Tennis goals: What 3 areas are you going to target?
- Fitness goals: What physical traits do you want to improve?
- Mental goals: What mental improvements are you going to make?
- Tactical goals: How are you going to incorporate your tennis changes into match play situations?

Day 2-5—Drills to incorporate new skills. Slow with plenty of instruction. Low to mid intensity.

Day 6—Rest day

Day 7-12—Drills to solidify new skills. Increasing difficulty with more game-like situations and conditions. Introduction of tactical elements to the tennis skills. Mid-high intensity.

Day 13-14—Rest 2 days

Day 15-21—Practice with peers or with coach as a hitting partner. Tennis skills now need to be tested under game-like speeds and with realistic bounces. Start with hitting drills and controlled point play situations. Slowly introduce difficult hitting drills and match play situations. Mid-high intensity with very high intensity days to push the limits of the new skills.

Day 22—Rest day

Day 23-30—Practice sets or a warm-up tournament or both. Coach is not as necessary but can help to make sure skills stay reinforced. The warm-up tournament can be a good chance to test the skills and is therefore not important to necessarily get good results, but instead to make sure the skills are working.

Big tournament (hopefully we do well)

Rest (3-5 days minimum)

Start all over!

SECTION 2:

TACTICAL

Showing adroit planning; aiming at an end
beyond the immediate action.

CHAPTER 4

EVALUATION

In this *Software* book (as opposed to the companion *Tennis Circuitry: Master the Hardware*), it is important to understand that there is a lot more "gray area" when it comes to software. Technique can be very black and white: either it is, or it isn't; it is rare for it to be in between. The same goes for the physical aspects of tennis. But tactics are unique in that there is room for individual interpretation. You cannot definitively say 100% of the time that one particular shot is always the right shot. You will often hear commentators say things like, "If they make the shot, they are a genius; if they miss it, they are an idiot." What they mean is that we are all too often judged unfairly in our tactical decision-making by whether the shot goes IN and WINS us the point. My goal is simply to identify what is good decision-making and what is bad decision-making. The player who tends to make more good decisions and limits bad or risky decisions will usually win the match if it is close in other ways. That is why good tactical decision-making is a must.

Strategy or Tactics?

These two terms can easily be confused. Strategy is more general and overarching. Strategically, you are a certain type of player, and you tend to do damage to your opponent in a certain way. For instance, my strategy is to be very aggressive with my court position, to come into the net often, and play very short points. Other strategies might be to stay back, play good defense, use a lot of counter-punching skills to keep the point going, and wear down the opponent mentally and physically. Regardless of the overarching strategy you use, you can be successful as a player.

Are you able to hit your forehand to all locations and with all the various amounts of spin, height, and power needed to break down your opponent?

Tactics are individual combinations of shots that happen within a point. Every strategy type will need to serve out wide, down the T, and in the body. Every strategy type will follow that up by using their weapon as often as possible and be able to hit that shot to the opponent's weakness. Every player will need to practice many multiple tactics for many different situations and it is here where we can make a big difference in our performance. Do not change your strategy, but within your strategy you will have many different tactical options that can be improved to make you a better competitor.

A good evaluation of tactics includes identifying any areas where a player is not confident or capable. For instance, can you hit down the line or cross court from every position and situation? If not, there is a tactical limit to your game that you will need to expand. If you can make the shot but when you're under pressure you get tight because you do not believe in your down the line or cross court, then that is also a problem.

A good evaluation will also determine where a player might be getting too obvious, such as only hitting cross court from a defensive backhand position. If you are too obvious with tactics your opponents will be able to figure you out.

Finally, a good evaluation will uncover whether these deficiencies are a result of software, and not hardware related. We are now talking about the decision-making process and not the physical abilities of the player. A tactical problem that is holding a player back would be a situation where the player is set up, ready to hit, has the technical ability to hit the proper shot, but then in match situations fails to make good decisions based on their tactical understanding. This would be different than someone lacking the technical ability to hit a certain type of shot. If you feel that physical ability is the issue, then you should consult the complement to this book, *Hardware*.

Many players are predictable when hitting defensive backhands.

How I do a good evaluation with my players

For a good tactical evaluation, you or your coach will need to see situations where you are playing weaker players, stronger players, and players of a similar level, as each of those will pose unique tactical challenges. It is also important to see situations where the competition has a variety of attributes. For example, playing fast and slow players, net players and baseline players, aggressive and defensive players. The more tactical situations you can observe the better you will be at identifying any weak areas in the decision-making process.

One of the many great things about the modern era is that video is so easily shared. I have worked with players remotely, many miles and even countries away, and worked with them to improve their tactics. All it takes is a video camera and some time and it's possible to watch matches from anywhere and begin to determine what areas could be improved tactically. For this reason, you should get as much match footage of yourself as possible, especially if it is of you in real tournament play, as those pressure packed moments will give clarity to your true ability. (Make sure your state, section, or country allows video recording, as some do not in tournament play. Always get your opponent's permission. Often, your opponent will be happy to allow it, especially if you share the video with them since it can be so valuable for tactical evaluation.)

Whether you use video or have your coach come see you play matches live and in person, I recommend compensating your coach for this time. It is easily as valuable—if not more valuable—than an hour-long technical lesson at the club. Having your coach witness you play will allow them to feel the stress you are feeling as it will be very difficult for any coach who really connects with their student to not get nervous right there with them. (I taught a girls' school where the #1 doubles team went to a tie-break set every match they played. The stress nearly gave me a heart attack—I was so freakin' nervous!)

I get nervous watching my players because I care about them and I am sure your coach cares about you as well.

When your coach is watching you play, or you yourself are watching you play, this is what you should be asking yourself:

Did I have a plan?

Did the plan make sense based on how the match progressed?

Did my plan match my strengths to their weaknesses?

Did I correctly identify weak areas in my opponent?

Can I do what is necessary to win against every type of opponent?

Do I know good tactics for every type of opponent?

Where do I typically break down in a point?

How can I disguise my weaknesses and stop my opponent from exploiting them?

Did my positioning on the court make sense for what I was attempting to do with the point?

Did my shot-selection make sense for where I was in the point?

Did my shot-selection ever go beyond my abilities or did I play within myself?

Did my physical or technical ability hold me back from executing a decent tactical plan?

CHAPTER 5

SERVING TACTICS

The serve and the return have been called the two most important shots in tennis, as they are the shots that get the point started. Yet, they have also been called the least practiced shots in tennis, with the return being under practiced no matter where you go. Why is it then if you go to a typical practice court around the country the majority of what you see being practiced is the regular old groundstroke?

While I cannot give you a definitive answer, I can speculate that it has something to do with what we perceive to be true versus what *is* true. If I asked you how long professional tennis players rally during their matches, what would you say? If you believe points are on the longer side, then it would make sense to practice all those regular groundstrokes as that would make up a large part of the points being played.

How often do rallies last between 0-4 shots, 5-8 shots, and 9+? (For this a 0 means 0 shots went in, or a double fault, a 1 would be a service ace or unreturnable serve because 1 shot went in, the serve, etc.)

Most people say something like, "40% for 0-4, 30% for 5-8, and 30% for 9+." If I asked tons of tennis fans, I would probably get ranges like 30-50% for 0-4, 30-50% for 5-8, and 20-35% for 9+.

That is what we *perceive* to be true based on our viewing experience and even our playing experience. We believe that rallies are typically on the longer end, and short points are not all that common. But what is the *reality?*

The reality is that far more points are actually very short, with close to 70% falling in the 0-4 range on average. Mid-range points are only 21% of tennis in the 5-8 rally length. And less than 10% of rallies last longer than 9+. This is SUPER DUPER important guys! This completely changes the way we view tactics, not to mention what we should be practicing tactically most of the time. It makes little sense to practice tactics that emphasize long rallies when they are *far less common.*

A serve being unreturned is the #1 thing that happens in tennis at all levels so a strong serve is a must.

What we should be emphasizing is how to win the short points more often. This makes even more sense when you consider that the statisticians went one step further on rally length. They found that the person who wins most of the short points (the 0-4 range), even if it is just a slight majority, goes on to win the match WAY MORE OFTEN! So not only are the short points the bulk of what happens in tennis, the person who wins more of those points goes on to win many more matches.

If you can get your opponent to return from the alley then you will be well set up to make them run on the next shot.

The problem is what we perceive. Our brains naturally gravitate towards those super interesting long rallies and we forget that we just saw the player serve twice and not a single ball came back over. We also instinctively know that to improve our strokes we need to hit them repeatedly (which we talked about earlier and is true). However, when we switch from the learning phase to the automation phase, we must start adding in the tactics behind the skill. It is far more common in tennis to hit a groundstroke immediately after a serve, which requires different footwork, happens at a different tempo, happens after using a continental grip, and happens with a different intent, than the types of ground-strokes hit in the 5-8 or 9+ ranges which happen far less often. This is an important distinction in the way we practice but, even more importantly, in the way we practice *tactics*.

That is why the tactical section of this book is broken down into serving and returning. And that is how we will, for the most part, be discussing tactics.

Serve location and how that impacts the next shot

Whether we are on the deuce side or the ad side there are three serve locations that we must consider: out-wide, down-the-T, and in-the-body. Out-wide has obvious implications for the next shot. Typically, after an out-wide serve, the shot that makes the most sense is to go to the now-open court on the other side. This will start the opponent off in the point by immediately running and defending. This is a favorite of professional tennis players and rightly so. It is so effective that even if you know it is coming you may very well be helpless to stop it. There is a natural follow-up to the out-wide/open court combo, which would be to hit *behind* the opponent. Hitting behind the opponent is a good change-up from going in front of them, which should realistically be the primary tactic after serving out-wide. Hitting behind will keep them honest and stop them from just sprinting to the open court immediately, preventing you from taking over the point as you should. Also, against a super-fast opponent you will find that going behind is uniquely effective because they can often run themselves back so fast to the middle to defend that open court space that their momentum can wrong foot them and they will be much slower going back into the corner from which they just came.

> So now for a little bit of that gray area...
> how the hell do you decide whether to
> go in front or to go behind?

There are some things you can watch for and some things that you will have to reason out for yourself. For instance, if you notice that your opponent has not yet recovered all the way to the middle, then they will have a much further distance to cover if you hit in front of them. This may be a wise play, unless of course they are running so fast to make up for the fact that they are not yet to the middle that they will not be able to change direction, in which case going behind them is the better play.

Unfortunately, you will have to use your best judgement and sometimes your judgement will be wrong. Sometimes your opponent will expect you to go in front of them and you will, while sometimes they will expect you to go in front of them and you won't. But here is the good news: It doesn't matter!

Sometimes this shot should go to the open court, but sometimes it has to go behind. This keeps our opponent honest.

The worst-case scenario is that you will need to turn a 0-4 rally into a 5-8 rally, and you will work the point a little longer until you can finish it off in a different way. Do not get frustrated if you hit in front of them and they were ready for it. That shift happens and *it ain't no thang*. If your serve and first shot are quality because all you were focused on was hitting the best shot possible, then it will probably still result in your winning the point. That is the power of being the server.

> ### As the server, you have a huge unfair advantage.

The next best option after serving out-wide would be to serve down-the-T. Down-the-T serves are beneficial to the server because going straight ahead is a shorter distance, giving your opponent less time to react. Not only that, the net is lower in the middle than on the sidelines so your flat serve, which will have a lower trajectory, has a good chance of making it over the net. Of course, the problem with the down-the-T serve is that it brings your opponent to the middle of the court, making it harder to force them out of position with the very first shot. This middle of the court position does have a benefit to the server, in that it is much harder to create angles from the middle of the court, meaning it is much easier to position yourself after the serve to hit a forehand, almost no matter what.

What do we do with that first forehand after a down-the-T serve?

What you do with that forehand is important, as it needs to have more purpose than the groundstroke hit after the out-wide serve. Since it will be difficult to hit a shot so well that it moves your opponent out of position laterally, what you can do with that first forehand is get your opponent out of position vertically, as in, backing them off the baseline with a shot that has good depth. The nice thing here is that you can go to either side and keep your opponent honest. Going deep to the backhand makes a lot of sense with this first shot, as it will force them to defend with their weaker stroke. This can lead to an easier short ball that you can then attack or get into an inside-out forehand to their backhand pattern, which we will talk about later.

Here is an idea that people do not often consider: hitting to their strength. This seems counter-intuitive because why the hell would I want to hit to the stronger forehand side? There are two reasons you should be willing to hit to both sides, and not always go to the backhand. First, if you hit to the forehand, you can get them out of position to the forehand which opens a lot more room to hit the next shot to the backhand. Modern players do not struggle as much with the backhand when in position as they have in the past but hitting a backhand while on the run will always be a challenge. There is nothing technically or physically that we can do as tennis players to change that. Second, the modern forehand is a complicated stroke and can take a little more time to execute. A strong shot from inside the baseline (like we might be expecting if having just hit a good serve and we got a shorter, easier reply) would rush the forehand into an error, or at least bring about more of a floater.

By taking their short ball and hitting it deep you can back them up to create more angles for the next shot.

Why would a forehand float more than a backhand when rushed?

The modern forehand has a ton of spin on it, over 2000 RPMs. While the forehand can be hit with a ton of power, typically when rushed, players keep the *spin* but lose the *power*. This is where we gain a huge edge, because a ball hit with a lot of spin but not too much power tends to "sit-up." When a ball is sitting up, it is moving slowly, and stays in a higher strike zone for a longer time. This makes it easy to load up and crush the ball from inside the baseline where we can easily hit winners or approach.

Taking the floater early and from up high will give you a distinct advantage on this shot.

The gray area: how will you know whether to hit to the forehand or backhand?

If your opponent has a very good forehand you may want to opt for more shots to the backhand, which should be the play you practice more often and is the play professionals use more often. If you notice that your opponent has a ton of spin but takes big swings at the ball, then think about going to the forehand side from time to time. Have you had a string of points where you went to the backhand right away and want to change it up? Don't be afraid to go to the strength. Once again, worst-case scenario, you would turn what would have been a 0-4 shot rally into a 5-8 shot rally and it will take you a tiny bit longer to set the point up. As I said before, this is the advantage of being the server. If the serve and the first shots are quality, you can basically guarantee that you will be ahead in the point and the sure favorite to win the point.

We all know that we should hit our spots on the serve, out-wide, open court, down-the-T, go for a big ace or get a short return. This is no big deal, basic stuff. Why the hell should you go in the body? Isn't that only for second serves? "I only go in the body when I was trying to go out-wide and I don't hit the serve good enough," chuckles John Isner as he hits career ace five *gagillion.*

Believe it or not, the body serve has some useful purposes that we should not ignore. Surprisingly, on the ad-side (for righties), for female professionals, the body serve is used more often than the out-wide! *WOAH, *mind blown.**

This makes sense if you understand a simple fact: Great competitors will keep doing the things that win them points. They don't care if it makes sense on paper, and when they get rewarded for something, they keep doing it. (This is also why a lot of people think lefties are better at spin than righties. There is nothing about being left-handed that allows us— yes, I am left-handed—from producing more spin. We are rewarded for it more than a righty would be, and so we keep doing it, while a righty tends to stop using it when they lose too many points.)

Female pros, as well as a lot of younger-development players on the way to the pros, tend to lack a good kick serve. The kick serve is what makes the out-wide serve so effective in singles. The kick serve continues to travel away from the backhand of a right-handed opponent and pushes them further out of position to their weaker side. However, without a good kick, you can accidentally create a serve that sits-up, like how forehands that have spin, but no power, sit up. This is a problem because even though your opponent is returning backhand, if it sits up you will get a rockin' return hit back at you. Plus, because you hit it out-wide, you gave them angles to work to make YOU run, which is not what you want when serving.

The gray area: to hit the body serve or not, that is the question. "Whether 'tis nobler in the mind to suffer the slings and arrows of outrageous misfortune, Or, to take arms against a sea of troubles, And by opposing end them. To DIE—to SLEEP—NO MORE!" (Sorry, I got carried away by the thought of Adam Sandler in *Billy Madison* reciting the *Hamlet* soliloquy. If you're too young to understand, just go on YouTube and look it up. It is worth it to see Adam Sandler at his best before he got old and bland.)

A body serve is a great option if you are still working on your kick serve and it just ain't kickin' yet, or if your opponent is using that out-wide angle to force you right back. If you aren't winning a good percentage of points on the ad-side, the body serve is worth trying. Also, a lot of players will try to cut off the out-wide angles by standing very close to the baseline. If you notice this, a good body serve will take away a lot of their time and could very easily jam them. This is also a great way to get them to back up so that you have more room to make them run on your out-wide shots. Then, finally, use the body serve as a change-up to get a good returner out of their rhythm. Most people practice moving *towards* the ball, but a body serve is hit *at* them, which forces them to move *away* from the ball, a counterintuitive move for some players.

Ahead in the point plays

Since we are talking about serving strategy, the assumption is that we will be ahead in the point after the serve and the first shot. Remember that being ahead in the point plays can happen when you are returning, they can happen immediately after the serve, or they can happen twenty shots deep in a rally. Regardless of when the play presents itself, once you are well enough ahead in the point, ramp up the pressure and inch yourself very close to finishing the point, if not outright ending it by happy accident.

Before we talk about specific plays, let's talk about how to identify that you are ahead in the point versus being neutral or behind. The best way to tell if you are ahead in the point is to observe your opponent. There are some telltale signs that your opponent is struggling; that is how we identify that we are ahead. Here is what to look for:

1. **Making contact out of the strike zone:** This is an educated guess, but usually you can tell when your shot is going to be far enough away from your opponent that it will do some damage and force them into a defensive shot. Examples of this would be making them run a very long distance, hitting a ball very high and heavy so they can't back up quickly enough, or

hitting a low biting slice so that they do not move up quickly enough.

2. **Hitting the ball very hard:** Hitting the ball very hard rushes your opponent into an uncomfortable position that can create a much softer, easier to attack shot. This could be because you hit such a good serve that you do not need to wait to set the point up. In that case, you can go straight to a play that will help you end the point. Sometimes you won't notice this happen until twenty balls into the rally. That is the joy and the frustration. Sometimes you will get it wrong. This is more of that gray area B.S. we keep encountering.

3. **Your opponent has a weakness and you hit to their weakness:** If you notice through the course of playing the match that your opponent has a weak shot somewhere in their game or some other flaw that is exploitable, and you happen to hit it there at any time during the point, you can now look for an opportunity to begin an ahead in the point play.

Sometimes, you will be able to begin an ahead in the point rally when you didn't do anything special at all. Sometimes your opponent will just inexplicably hit a softer, safer shot by accident. But here is the golden rule that I want you to remember:

Frequently, you will have an opportunity in the point where you could begin executing an ahead in the point play that will lead to you potentially winning the point. The problem is that if you pass up that opportunity, the next opportunity may be your opponent's, and the better they are the less likely they will pass it up the way you did. It is better to cash in your chips while you are ahead and be the first to execute an ahead in the point play, especially since we know that most points in tennis are on the shorter side.

Thinking in 3D can help you get it out of their strike zone, not just left/right, but also up/down and front/back.

Attacking the high ball

We talked a little bit earlier about how the modern game of tennis has an ample amount of topspin, and that topspin without power can sit-up. We already talked about how that shot allows you more time to load up and hit hard, not to mention that if you make contact up higher you get a better angle. This way when you do hit it hard it has better margin than hitting hard from a lower contact point.

But what do you do next? Do you see that when you hit the ball hard from up high that your opponent is rushed, or do you see that you hit it nicely in the corner and it is out of their strike zone? What's next?

Traditional tennis tactical philosophy would tell you that you should close into the net and volley. While that is certainly an option, be open to other ideas. Typically, if you are attacking this type of shot, you could be a little far back in the court and not really in a great position to come to the net. Plus, players today can still generate ample power when they're out of position. If you are not an accomplished volley player, you may end up botching the net shot and letting them back in the point.

Another option is to adopt a more aggressive court position and take the next shot early. Adopting an aggressive court position may mean standing inside the baseline slightly, or it may just mean being super-ready to jump on the short ball. Basically, you are assuming the next shot coming back will be slower or hit more to the middle where you can reasonably take the ball early and it not be as risky. If you do this the right way, they will still be stuck in the corner recovering while you are hitting the next shot to the open court. If they manage to hit the ball deep, you would simply take it out of the air as a swinging volley as it will not be hit as hard because they're out of position.

Another way of thinking about this would be to call it a "delayed approach." Instead of approaching off the first good shot you hit, hitting one good shot to the corner, you would take the next ball very early where, now that you are in closer, it will be much easier to get to the net. When you do this, your opponent will be just that much farther out of position, which can take the pressure off your volley. (In all likelihood, your volley is probably not good enough given the general lack of volley skills being practiced nowadays. Don't be offended, I'm just callin' it like I see it, folks.)

Traditional approach shot

If your opponent is out of position, another common thing to happen is for their ball to land short in the court. Because they were out of position, they could not create the depth to keep you back, or they lost so much power that the ball landed short. Either way, for this type of shot the ball will not be sitting up high like in the previous example but will instead be in a more normal strike zone location. Traditional approach shots can be of the sliced or topspin variety and what you want is to force your opponent into a difficult position. Since you are in closer and your opponent is slightly out of position, that means you should be able to do this with a normal amount of power. From this difficult position, your opponent should only have two choices: hit a very defensive shot, one where you should easily be able to put the point away or go for a difficult aggressive shot from out of position to attempt to win the point.

I like this play for a couple of reasons. Most people believe that frequently approaching the net is an aggressive strategy. Putting pressure on your opponent is considered being aggressive (which has the connotation of being risky). Here is why I just don't buy that: *there is nothing difficult about hitting a traditional approach shot.* Your opponent screwed up by hitting it short or soft. While you may be taking away their time and being "aggressive" by following it into the net, you are not hitting a risky shot. A traditional approach can be relatively normal and your inside the baseline court position helps to take care of the rest. If you practice your approach shots, you will not have to take on any unnecessary risk to hit them.* (Big asterisk here since most people do not practice this enough. Make sure you do!)

Traditional approaches can be sliced, hit with topspin, or hit flatter if up high enough.

Your opponent, on the other hand, will have to hit it harder than a normal shot or else you will be able to volley it to the open court with no problem. They will also have to hit it closer to the sideline because a hard shot hit right at the volley isn't difficult either. They will also be doing this from out of position (sometimes 10-15 ft behind the baseline). You are using a low-risk tactic, while transferring a lot of risk onto your opponent. That's what a winning tennis tactic looks like in a nutshell.

A word about volleying

In *Hardware*, I talk about thinking smarter (angles) not harder (power) when at the net. When you hit an approach shot or come to the net, look for ways to get your opponent farther out of position than they already are, and don't try to hit through them to blast a volley winner. This is very different from what most people will tell you about coming to the net so don't be fooled. The moment you decide to go for a WINNER your whole demeanor will change, and you will instinctively hit closer to the lines or harder than necessary to win the point. This could lead to you missing easy shots when you were ahead in the point, which is not a good combination.

This doesn't make sense for when you are at the net. You would never be up at the net when you are super behind in the point (unless of course your opponent hits a deft drop shot), and it doesn't make sense to take on extra risk. If you are that far ahead in the point, you want to make sure you go on to win the point. Going for a WINNER makes it more likely that you will lose the point when you should have won it, and that double blow can kill the psyche of any tennis player. It is often what swings matches. (We'll discuss this concept further in the mental section of the book coming up next. STAY TUNED!)

Volleying should be about making their passing shot as difficult as possible, not necessarily going for the winner. Winners become a happy accident.

If your opponent comes up with an amazing shot and ends up winning the point when they were way behind, then guess what, who cares! You made them do something exceptional to win. If you continue to structure points in this way, you will win a higher percentage of those points than they will. Since we can't possibly win every point, the least we can do is make the points our opponent manages to win as difficult as possible.

Make them run

"Make them run" plays are better for more defensive styled players, but everyone should have them in their arsenal. Let's say you are not super-comfortable coming to the net and would rather stay on the baseline, yet you still want to be aggressive. That is where make them run plays come in, and there are multiple ways to do them. With a make them run play you want to push them even farther out of position than they already are until they are so far out of position that you safely hit a winning shot, or they miss.

Hitting a drop shot is likely the most overused version of the make them run play. Yes, the drop shot will make your opponent run, but a poorly executed drop shot can put your opponent right back into a position where they are in control. Try to be strategic when you're attempting a drop shot. It helps if you can wrong-foot your opponent by hitting it behind them or having them on their heels expecting you to hit hard and instead you hit soft (this is called disguise). Make sure they are not expecting it because if they get to the drop shot early enough, they can take over the point (They will expect this play if you do it too often or are too obvious about when you use it, so don't overuse it.)

Another good make them run option is to hit an angle. When your opponent has hit the ball soft and short, you will be in more control over the shot and can safely angle the ball and make them run off the court. Angles work well because even if they get it back, they will be so far off the court that recovering is going to be nearly impossible. Then it will be that much easier to take the ball early and go in front of them, go behind them and wrong foot them, approach, or even drop shot as ways to finish the point.

The last make them run play is to slice and dice them. This is not used as often nowadays as many players do not have that variety. The players who do reap a lot of benefit from it. You can use a slight side-spin to add some off the court movement to a good down the line slice. Now, not only will they be running, but they are also going to be digging down low for the ball. This will make it less likely that they can play good defense. You can also hit an angled shot as a slice. The angled slice shot is often called a "bait" shot because it makes your opponent think they have no option but to approach as they will be running up and into the court to retrieve it. If they fall for the bait and you have brought them into the net on your terms instead of theirs, it is much easier to pass or lob them.

> **If you're ahead in the point, I do not recommend these moves but they do happen.**

The following are shot selection choices that you will see in the pros and they do have their place. These shot selection options have a lower probability of success, so if possible, stick to the other options listed. Please and thank you.

Modern approach shots

The traditional approach shot is not used as much as the modern approach shot which is a real shame. Right now, most professionals just do not believe in their volley abilities enough to risk having to hit one. Instead of hitting a traditional approach (which makes it more likely they will have to volley), they go for the modern approach (where the ball coming back is less likely, so no volley skill is needed). The modern approach takes a mid-court ball that was hit lower or slower and attempts to hit it from in closer AND much harder.

These approach shots are riskier than the traditional approach because they have added speed from a disadvantageous angle. The only benefit to this option is that because the ball is hit so much harder, the resulting volley, should the ball come back, will be easy enough that it will not stress anyone into an error. This is a great option if you are still working on your volleys and do not feel confident in them yet, or if you are playing an opponent who is phenomenal at passing shots. Yes, sometimes you will have a good strategic reason to pass up the traditional pass and just hit it hard. My advice is to make the traditional version work first, and then go the modern route should the opponent or situation tell you that a traditional approach just won't get it done.

Pull the trigger

I am not fond of this tactic, but even this one has its place. Pulling the trigger just means to go for the big shot, essentially a winner, from the back of the court. This type of shot

If you are sitting on a coin flip and deciding whether to go for it, it's probably best to wait for a better opportunity that has odds that will work in your favor.

is best left to those who have a considerable weapon in their groundstrokes. If your groundstroke is good enough to hit it so hard that your opponent will not be able to get it, then the "grip it and rip it" approach can sometimes work. Remember that by attempting this you will be taking on considerable risk, hitting the ball harder and much closer to the line. This type of play should be left for when the incoming shot is easy enough that you can execute it at better than 50%. If you are only sitting at a 50-50 split, then there is no payout for going for it and you should just continue rallying.

Just hope they miss

There are some days when nothing is working. The groundstrokes are misfiring, you're lucky if the volley doesn't hit your side of the net first, and you just can't seem to win a point. There is still the option of at least *not losing* the point. Tennis has a funny scoring system that way. My score will advance if my opponent makes a mistake. For this tactic, do not try to go further ahead in the point if you are ahead in the point. Instead, just try to stay a tiny bit ahead in the point (never advancing but never retreating).

There is a unique kind of pressure that happens when you as a player are not making mistakes and force your opponent to come up with the goods. This strategy can also be used by players who are defensive in nature. If you make enough shots, and you stay incrementally ahead in the point, you still have a decent chance that your opponent will miss, and you keep the percentage edge that you need. Even if your edge is only 51%, you can still win a match that way. This strategy comes with a disclaimer. If you are in an offensive situation, then offense is what you should play. There are plenty of times in tennis where defense is needed, but if you become *so* defensive that you can't manage to stay ahead in the point and you let them back in, then you are not making good tactical decisions. When you never try to get further ahead in the point, it makes it easier for your opponent to turn their own defense back into offense. Be careful when using this tactic, as it is a tightrope act that can backfire.

CHAPTER 6

RETURN OF SERVE TACTICS

Tennis is a game of errors. No matter what level you play, more points are lost from errors than are won from winners or even the good shots that force the mistake. What do you think the number one error is that is made on the pro tour? Backhand return of serve. Not only are the majority of serves hit to the backhand because it is typically the weaker side, it is such a weakness that players miss this shot more than any other. That is important, because you give yourself a HUGE edge if all you do is get the ball back in play. (Basically, there are no tactics or strategy without consistency. If you can't get the ball back in the court, your only tactic is to get the ball in play.)

Remember how I said earlier that the server has a big advantage and is virtually guaranteed to win the point? The returner can take the server's big advantage and turn it into an even split by getting the first two balls back in play. Once those first two shots go in, the advantage that the serve has is completely diminished. It becomes a feed the ball in underhanded and play it out rally point. Before we talk about strategy, let's talk about ways to get more returns back into play and give ourselves enough chances to even out the playing field.

Return positioning

Positioning on the return of serve can give you an edge because it is one of the only ways you can manipulate the situation when your opponent is serving. Of course, when you adjust the depth of your positioning you have a trade-off. The farther back you stand, the slower the ball will be moving when it gets to you. (For every 10 feet that you back off the baseline, the ball will be moving approximately 5 MPH slower.) The trade-off is that you would have to do more running to cover a well-placed serve with some movement. The closer in you stand, the easier it is to cut off the angle on wide serves and you can take time away from the server; however, you will be sacrificing time to react and time to swing so it can be more challenging in that sense. The good news is that you can have success with either option. Nadal likes to stand far back even on hard courts where it is typical to stand in close. Federer likes to return from in close, and he has even used that in close position to immediately begin attacking his opponent.

My best suggestion would be to experiment with both. See which one you prefer, and which gives you the best results. You may find that on clay you are better off back and on a hard court in, and that is fine. You may even find that you start a match farther back, and then slowly go in as you gain confidence. It's really all good, if you keep in mind that you do not have to do anything special with the return, but you do need to continue making as many returns as possible.

Stand farther back for extra time, stand closer in to take away time, and on 2nd serve look to use your forehand!

Slice vs. Topspin

Another stylistic difference that returners have is whether they tend to chip or slice the return, versus come over the top of it or hit a topspin return. The advantage of a sliced return is that it takes less time to execute. Obviously the more stretched you are on the return, the more likely it will be that you are forced to slice. A sliced return can also stay low off the bounce which may make it more difficult for your opponent to attack immediately, like what I talk about with the volley and slicing and dicing tactics. The advantage of a topspin return is that it is more likely this aggressive return will force your opponent off balance. The topspin on this shot will make your return powerful if you connect cleanly. The topspin can bring the ball down safely for you. The interesting thing about this stylistic difference is that, just like return position, you can do either and be fine, and you can mix it with the return position differences we talked about and any combination has the potential to work.

Wawrinka likes to chip the return from far back, while Federer likes to do so from further in. Nadal likes to return with topspin from far back, while Djokovic likes to from closer in. You can even have differences in slice or topspin from forehand to backhand. (Obviously more players slice their backhand than forehand.)

You can even adjust from first to second. If you like to stand back and slice on first, go for it; if you like to stand back and hit topspin on second, you can, or you can stand in close for second. There are so many combinations and all of them work if you understand two fundamental ideas. One, you need to make a lot of returns, and the second shot after the return brings you to a neutral spot in the rally. Two, while you want to be more aggressive on the second serve return, you do not need to hit super hard, or even close to the lines, to gain an advantage in the rally early on.

A word on the return of serve footwork:

In *Hardware,* I talk about the footwork, particularly the split-step. The split-step is SUPER important on the return of serve. Even the best returners in the world will struggle against a bad server at the very beginning of the match because they need to adjust their timing of the split-step. Every server has a slightly different tempo and slightly different timing to their toss and contact point. Once you have that timing down, you should be able to return the serve easily.

TO BE CLEAR, I did *not* say that the best returners start returning better when they start reading the serve better. This makes it sound as if they can figure out where the serve is going before it is struck. While some bad servers have tells and tendencies, the best returners are the best, not because they *read* well, but because they get in and out of their *split-step* so well. When the best returners return, they are not turning their hips *before* contact (reading); they are turning their hips while they are *in the air* on their split, as they are seeing which way the ball is going and they are going that direction. They are NOT guessing! DO NOT GUESS!

If you feel the need to guess which way the ball is going then something is seriously wrong with your return of serve footwork. Better to wait and see where it is going and then go there.

After the split-step you may have time to do what some call a "transfer step" where you transfer your weight forward out of an open stance. You may be stuck stretching more and doing an open stance with a "mogul step" as some call it, where you hop off your outside foot and land on your outside foot again. You may be stretched so far wide that you must hit off your outside leg and then bring your inside leg across before you can recover. All the steps are situational and all of them are necessary to learn, but if you just put yourself in enough matches and return enough serves you will most likely figure them out on your own. If you feel like your return footwork sucks, then consider reading *Hardware* and learning more about footwork or consulting with a knowledgeable coach.

Pros and Cons of Targeting Forehand vs. Backhand

Often on the second serve return you will have the ability to aim, even if minimally. Pro tour statistics indicate that most of the time the return is targeted down the middle or a little more towards the backhand side. The reason the return is hit deep down the middle is because it is still a return of serve, and we are not in an ideal situation to be hitting ground strokes like normal just yet. However, you should at least be able to go a little more towards the forehand or backhand.

It's easy to think that the backhand is the weaker side and that is why returns go there more often, but there are additional considerations. If you are the type of returner who likes to stand in closer for a second serve return, you may gain an advantage by going to the forehand side at least part of the time. The modern forehand with all its power still has a weakness because it can be rushed and will create a spin-heavy shot that does not have enough power and will sit up. It is even easier to do this on return of serve and most people don't realize it. Directly after a serve, the server will be standing inside the court as that is how loading the legs transfers into the serve. With you standing in close, and them having not recovered to their ideal baseline position, a good deep return may rush the forehand into an error, or at least a very attackable ball. Vice versa, some players develop a strong redirect backhand, and simply hitting it hard and deep may not do as much damage as you may have hoped. You will need to do some discovery in the early phases of a match to determine how you can best get into return games.

If you can rush the forehand it can sometimes be more effective than rushing the backhand.

Behind in the point plays

You got the return back in play. GREAT! Now you are running for dear life and you have no idea what to do next. You are behind in the point, and typically will be after getting the return back…

… but that's OK.

Notice that I have not divided this section into the idiocy that is stereotypical player types. "Oh, if you are a counter-puncher you will play like this, but if you are an aggressive baseliner, you'll do this, and if you are a serve and volley player, um, I don't know what you will do because those don't exist anymore."

HOGWASH!

Have you noticed how Nadal is often stepping into the court and ripping forehands? Pretty weird for a "counter-puncher." What about how Stan Wawrinka, the epitome of aggressive baseliner, chips the return and plays plenty of defense? That doesn't jive with the player types model, and that is because that stuff just doesn't work anymore.

Everyone must defend on return of serve.

If you try to attack right away, you will make too many errors and never get a decent shot at a break of serve.

Everyone must attack...

...or at least be comfortable attacking after a good first serve.

Tennis is now less about a type of player, and more about understanding situations and making an appropriate decision based on your strengths and weaknesses. Sure, Nadal is a very good defensive player, and yes, Wawrinka is a very good offensive player, but they are not one-sided, nor do they make stereotypical decisions. There are even some US Opens where Nadal was super-aggressive, and some where he was super-defensive. This happened in the same tournament, with the same surface, but on various years he either didn't have the same kind of confidence, or the conditions did not reward certain types of plays. You had better have some good defense *and* some good offense if you want to win in this game.

High and heavy

A heavy ball is when the ball has enough spin and enough power that it does not sit up, but instead bounces up aggressively and pushes the opponent back. Hitting it hard and accurately becomes a challenge for anyone in this situation. A high and heavy ball will go up high, creating a lot of air time. This air time allows you, the player behind in the point, to make your way back to the middle of the court where your opponent has been trying desperately to move you from.

Also, a high and heavy ball will typically make the opponent back up to hit it, because taking a ball like that directly after the bounce is challenging. With your opponent backed up, it will be challenging for them to hit the ball hard enough to create a clean winner. If they are not accurate enough thanks to your high and heavy shot, you will be able to regain a footing in the point and can begin looking for opportunities to use your ahead in the point plays.

High and heavy shots have become so frequently used that you should come up with a go-to strategy for how to handle this type of play. If you are ahead in the point, you should expect your opponent will try something like this to get back in the point. Your options are to Federer the ball and half volley it or let it get up a little and take it from up high, like what we talked about in the ahead in the point plays. This one will not be sitting up and therefore will be slightly more difficult. Alternately, you could move forward and take the ball out of the air. Whatever you decide to do, try your best not to back up too often, as that is exactly what your opponent wants you to do. If you are the behind in the point person, when you see your opponent backup, that is signal that your defense worked.

There is a big difference between your opponent hitting on the baseline and hitting 10 feet behind it.

Slice it low and slow

A good slice is like pure gold. The slice has many wonderful benefits if you are behind in the point. For starters, you can contact a slice a little later and it doesn't require as much time to execute, so it works well when you are rushed, either because they made you run like crazy or because they hit it hard. A slice will float through the air. It ends up going further and doesn't require as much power. It's great for when you are running so much you can't wind up and hit your topspin hard (attempting to may just end up creating a ball that sits up anyway).

To me, the best part about a slice is its potential to stay low off the bounce. Obviously if you hit a slice too high, it will bounce up high and sit up like crazy, but if you keep

From down low, a lot of players will fail to hit as high a quality of a shot making the slice a great defensive option.

it low, it will bounce nice and low. This forces your opponent to get down slightly out of their strike zone and attack from a position where they have less margin for error. Also, a slice has less power, which may seem like a bad thing, but often players struggle to generate their own power and prefer using a little bit of power from their opponents shot. Finally, a slice offers a nice change from the constant topspin that most players hit. The downside is if you hit too many slices consecutively. Then your opponent will have an easier time figuring out your low and slow shot.

Down the middle, cross-court, or down-the-line

When it comes to playing defense, most coaches have two strategies. One is that hitting the ball down the middle keeps the ball away from the lines and that makes it a very safe shot. The second defensive theory revolves around using your cross courts which is supposed to be a higher percentage due to the net being lower and the court being longer. While these are fine ideas, they do not match what is happening on the pro tour. The truth is there are pluses and minuses to all the different shot combinations, and it is perfectly acceptable to hit certain shots down the line, especially if you understand why you may want to do so, contrary to the warnings of tennis coaches everywhere. Let's dissect each tactic so you know what your options are.

Cross-court

Cross-court, the net is lower by 6 inches, and the court is longer by 4.5 feet. These are two important reasons why going cross court can benefit you, but that leaves out the single most important benefit to going cross court, which is that you as the person hitting will not have to recover as far to be in a decent position to defend. Because of geometry (that middle-school motherfudger is back to bite you), you will have to recover much further if you hit down the line. If you are already defending and now you are hitting yourself even further out of position, NO BUENO! (maybe I learned more from my years of Spanish than I thought).

This makes it sound like cross court is a good idea while defending. While it is a good option, there are of course some downsides. Let's say that your defense causes you to hit the ball a little short or a little soft. A good approach shot strategy is to hit the ball down the line. You would be setting your opponent up perfectly for this if you hit it short and cross-court. Another problem is that you are hitting it closer to the sideline by aiming cross-court. People often fail to recognize that angles beget angles, meaning that if you hit a good cross-court, but out of a defensive situation, it may make it easier for your opponent to hit an even better angle and make you run like crazy. Finally, most players are told to hit cross-court in defense, and an intelligent player will be waiting on that, expecting it even. While it is a smart play, if you only hit in that way, you are too predictable. It can give your opponent a time and movement advantage, as they can get into position faster and have more time to execute the shot.

Down-the-middle

Old tried and true, down-the-middle. Hitting down-the-middle is possibly the safest of the defensive shot selection choices you have, as you will be aiming as far from either sideline as possible. Like hitting the ball cross-court, recovery demands are not high, and you will not be going over the tall part of the net into the shortest part of the court. There is another benefit to hitting down-the-middle that many don't realize. This is mostly true when hitting deep or hard down the middle, but how often do we practice moving out of the way of the ball? If you are like most people you will do most of your drilling practicing running towards the ball and seldom will you practice getting out of its way. If you use the down-the-middle to test the movement of your opponent, it can often be more effective than hitting to a side. (This is especially true of fast players who almost seem to enjoy being on the run.)

While hitting cross-court creates angles that beget angles, down-the-middle does not. That is just one more reason why down-the-middle can be effective. You give your opponent no angles to exploit. They will have to hit through you to win the point. Combine a good down-the-middle with a low slice with no pace and you can easily turn defense back into offense. The downsides of down-the-middle should be obvious. If you don't make your opponent run and you end up accidentally hitting the ball soft or short, you are basically asking them to tee off on the ball. Good luck playing defense when that happens.

Down-the-line

It seems like hitting the ball down-the-middle or cross-court are solid bets. If I know anything about percentages you can't possibly have three choices, two of which are good options, and then the third one is too. Does that mean hitting down-the-line is for suckers? Not so fast.

There are reasons why hitting down-the-line in defensive situations is useful but remember that this comes with a big old asterisk. If you hit down the line, you are inviting your opponent to make you run more if you are not careful. When you hit down the line, you create the longest recovery distance possible for yourself. Furthermore, if you combine this with your opponent hitting shallow angles cross-court off your down-the-line, you will be off to the races. (Alarm bells should be going off in your head right now. YES, if your opponent hits down-the-line you should answer with a good shallow angle cross-court.)

However, there are some great benefits to hitting down-the-line. My favorite tactical reason for hitting down-the-line when I am behind in the point is to change the direction of the rally. Often rallies are exchanged cross-court to cross-court, because that is the high percentage nature of the shot combined with the mechanical nature of the human body and how we generate power on groundstrokes.

As an example, let's say that I am the weaker player in a forehand-to-forehand cross-court rally on the deuce court, but I feel I have an advantage in the cross-court to cross-court rally backhand-to-backhand on the ad side. I can use a down-the-line shot to bait my opponent into hitting the ball to my backhand and getting the rally out of the pattern that favors them. If you use a good high-heavy or even a slice to initiate this change of direction, it should make it difficult for your opponent to hit that shallow angle cross-court shot that makes the down-the-line so risky. While most coaches will tell you down-the-line is a super risky low percentage shot when on defense, I find that it is useful in many defensive situations and should be a part of your tactical decision-making.

If all else fails, lob

The lob is an underutilized shot. I love the lob. Some players look down on it, as if to say, "I am above needing to use a lob." Well, that's just silly. Every point is worth the same regardless of how hard you had to work for it. The benefits of the lob are numerous. The lob stays in the air for a long time, giving you the ability to regain your good positioning if your opponent forced you far off the court. The lob will also bounce up off the court fast and high. This can make it challenging for your opponent to set up to hit a decent forehand if you give your lob forward momentum, such as a topspin lob. A backspin lob will move even slower than a normal shot and can sometimes "dance" around in the wind, making it challenging to return. A lob gives little pace for your opponent to work with and can be tricky for those who have trouble generating their own pace. A lob can also bait your opponent into going for too much and they may end up over hitting.

The higher the level, the less often the lob pays off, yet professional tennis players still opt for the lob when all else fails. That is because of the "just make them hit one more ball" mentality. When you make your opponent hit just one more shot every single point, it does a couple things. Psychologically, you are sending the signal to your opponent that their best groundstroke or volley will not win them the point. This can make your opponent go for just a little more on the next groundstroke or volley. This type of defense also

Get them to "blink" and miss this shot and you will gain a psychological edge.

gives your opponent plenty of time to think. For some reason, when we are given a little extra time to think as tennis players, we tend to think about the wrong thing (namely, whether we will win the point or not). If you can get your opponent to blink, so to speak, and they accidentally miss the overhead, you will get more than just one point.

That is because we know we are supposed to make that overhead. When we miss an easy shot such as an overhead, especially when we believe that we should have won the point, it can turn into the moment a match changes from one player in control to the other. Plenty of matches have turned on one point that player A thought they should have won that player B goes on to win. Even if your opponent just hits every lob for an overhead winner, at least you will keep asking that difficult question, "Will this be the one shot where they make a fatal mistake?"

Behind in the point plays I do not recommend

Blast it

I know what players are thinking when they try this, "I am behind in the point. I have a low chance of winning this point anyway. I might as well go for it and hope for the best." That is a dangerous way to think. Essentially, you are giving up on the point AND on yourself. You are giving up on the point because you have decided that, instead of attempting to come back from behind in the point, you would rather just go for a huge winner with a slim probability of success. You are giving up on yourself because you are performing as if you do not believe that you can fight your way back into the point.

It's unfortunate when this tactic ends up working because it is rewarding one of the dumbest things you can do as a player. Are there times when you should do it? Absolutely, but I hesitate to identify those times because I do not want you to think that it is a good idea. When might it be? Let's say you are starting to feel tired, and you need to conserve energy for a more important moment in the match. Going for the blast the moment you get behind in the point will stop you from having to waste any energy in the pursuit of a defensive outcome to the point.

But here is the thing that most people do not realize about that type of thinking: what if you could have won that point by playing defense? What if by going for it and ultimately missing, because you will most of the time, you end up making the match go on longer? Didn't you end up creating more work for yourself in the name of conserving energy? This also happens when players stop moving their feet when they are tired. All you are doing is creating more work for yourself in the long run by not giving that effort in the present. If you fight for every point and win the points you are capable of winning, ultimately the match will be over in your favor quickly, or you will at least made it as difficult as possible for your opponent to win.

Bring them in

This one is not so bad as blasting it, but it is not something I would recommend for when you are behind in the point.

Players nowadays are bad at volleys and usually do not practice their approach game as much as they should. But, and this is a *big but (Kardashian-sized even)*, there is a huge difference between when you are in control of the point and bring the opponent in on YOUR terms, as opposed to when you are behind in the point and try to bring them in. Normally, when players are ahead in the point, they expect a shorter ball and are waiting on it. This is one of the few times in tennis when players usually do a good job of approaching because it is from a situation that they are comfortable with and have practiced. However, just like with everything we have discussed, there are certainly times when it can work out. If their volleys are terrible, then bring them in and watch them swat at air. Also, some players just have a knack for passing shots. If you are one of those people (I hate you), you will certainly find an advantage in having them at the net as you will have an opportunity to pass.

Finally, here is one more way to end a point relatively quickly. If you bring them in, either you are going to pass, or they are going to hit a winning volley or overhead. At least it can be over quickly. Some players benefit from keeping rallies short. Players can get into a groove if you allow them to hit plenty of groundstrokes. If you are an aggressive player who wants to keep rallies short to stop your opponent from getting into a groove, then this could be part of your overall strategy.

Although I've talked about a bunch of tactics, I didn't even get into specifics. THIS IS WHY YOU NEED A DAMN COACH! A coach will help you identify different tactics, specific directions, and the overall strategy that will work best for you. Every opponent is unique and will require a specific blend of the right tactics for you to be successful. Make sure you practice as many options as possible. If you only have a small well of options, then when you come up against the one opponent who requires a different set of tactics you will be sunk.

This keeps tennis interesting long-term. The Bryan brothers are notorious for reinventing their tactical choices every few years because all their opponents study them and start to figure them out. Federer has had an amazing resurgence now that he is over 35 thanks to his ability to try out different tactics, namely slicing less against certain opponents (Nadal). While Federer could still slice frequently and win against someone like Del Potro (who seems to hate bending his knees to get down for those low slices), Federer saw that he needed other options for the people he would be playing against in the finals of grand slams. He practiced those options against the rank and file of the tour until he felt confident enough in them to do them against the best of the best (just like we covered in the practice section first thing in this book).

SECTION 3:

MENTAL

Of or relating to the total emotional and
intellectual response of an individual
to external reality.

CHAPTER 7

EVALUATION

It takes a good mental approach to practice correctly and to be diligent enough to go to the gym and take that part of your training seriously. It takes smart decision-making to use good tactics. It will take some serious will-power to be a professional tennis player. But beyond those more obvious mental components, there are some incredibly valuable mental skills that we should work on to achieve our fullest potential on the court. Just like before, a solid evaluation can help you understand which components may be lacking and what the best pathway is to improve those areas.

When we play a tennis match that lasts for an hour and a half, how much of that tennis match do you think is spent hitting the ball? Most people grossly overestimate the reality. It is not uncommon for actual match play to be under 15 minutes during an hour and a half match. That means a huge part of tennis is the time in between points, the rest periods. Mental coaches report that the player who wins will win because of the way they use that time. A huge part of the mental game of tennis is understanding how to best use rest periods to help us mentally focus when the actual point is being played.

Going to the towel, fixing your strings, and having good rituals like bouncing the ball are all effective mental habits for staying process-oriented.

Another important part of a mental evaluation is looking at process-oriented versus result-oriented thinking. When tennis players become too result-oriented, they start to become distracted by those thoughts and cannot focus on the task at hand. We are not in control over whether we win or lose. Thinking about it will only make us stressed, emotional, or nervous. The best cure for this is to be process-oriented in our thinking. Process-oriented is when we think about the actions required to execute a shot or tactic. Making sure that we do the correct footwork is something that we ARE in control over, that does lead to increased success in the point, and is therefore process-oriented. This part of the mental game becomes a catch-22, "I want to win so I think about winning but that makes me lose. Instead, I should think about hitting the ball correctly, but if I hit the ball correctly so that it will go in, I will win, but if I think about that, I will lose." Starting to see how difficult the mental game can be?

Finally, the way we talk to ourselves has a huge effect on our mental well-being during a tennis match. I recently heard a great question that perfectly sums up what good self-talk should be. Ask yourself this question, "Would I be friends with someone if they talked to me the way I talk to myself when I play?" We chastise ourselves so many times over our mistakes, and it truly is self-destruction on the tennis court. A good mental approach to the game will include self-talk strategies to bolster your emotional state and allow you to focus on the task at hand instead of overly focusing on the missed shots that happened in the past.

How do I conduct a mental evaluation?

One nice thing about the mental evaluation is that I do not have to witness it to understand what is happening. In fact, I find the best method for identifying mental issues is by asking the right questions:

- Do you think that you are performing as well in your matches as you do in practice?
- Do you tend to miss easy shots during certain moments, such as if the game or set is on the line?
- Do you perform better when you have the lead or when you are behind in the score?
- Do you perform better when you are playing someone who is worse than, better than, or just as good as you?
- Do you get angry, nervous, distracted, overwhelmed, frustrated, or generally lose focus when you are playing?

You will notice that all these questions hint at a mental problem and not a physical, tactical, or technical problem. What is great about this is that no matter your skill level, improving your mental game will allow you to live up to your CURRENT potential. Many players fail to realize how excellent they could be if they would only make the shots they *can* make, because their mental game causes them to miss those (seemingly easy) shots.

Let's be nice to ourselves and not make tennis any harder than it already is.

How can you go about doing a mental evaluation?

There is a saying in sports psychology that some of the best sports psychologists are the coaches themselves. While there might be some truth to that, more often coaches hurt the players' mental game instead of helping it. What do I mean by this? It is easy to observe once you know the signs. For instance, the player should be process-oriented, not result-oriented. Yet, most coaches are overly result-oriented.

Here is a good test. Watch any coach give a lesson. They will usually have a goal for the drill. If there is no goal, that is an even bigger red flag, but let's assume there is a goal because most coaches will at least get that right. The goal should be to practice what is instructed on and not the result (forehand technique instead of just getting it "in"). Watch for long enough and you will see a few tell-tale signs that the coach is more interested in the results. If the coach looks back into the court to see if the ball went in, then they are focused on the results. If the coach is just mindlessly counting how many times the shot went in, then the coach is overly focused on results. If the coach only says, "good shot" when the ball goes in, especially if the player did not achieve the goal of the drill, then they are overly focused on the results.

A good coach gives feedback on the *process*. Let's say you are working on your forehand technique. You could do it correctly and still miss (after all, Roger Federer has perfect technique and still misses). The coach should let you know by saying, "That was correct. Next time just aim a little higher," or something to that effect. As mastery of the change occurs, the focus can slightly shift to the ball going in, but that should not become the focus of the drill. Priority should still be given to performing it correctly according to the standards of the drill's goal.

Coach needs to stay process oriented just like you do as a player. Find a coach who models proper mental skills as that will make it easier for you to adopt them as well.

When you evaluate your own mental game, make sure you are doing so with good guidance. Parents and coaches can sometimes be negative mental influences if they are overly result-oriented in their own thinking. If you have a coach who fits the bill, then great, have them watch your matches and give you feedback on how well you did. Of course, you can show them video of your matches if they cannot attend.

They should be looking for how well you stuck to your process goals, how well you utilized the in between point time, how well you controlled your emotions, and how well you focused in key moments. Then go back to the practice section of the book. Incorporate your mental changes into a training block, come up with a plan for improving one aspect of your mental game, and be diligent in your mental practice.

Story time

I had a student named Mike who was a technically sound player but felt he was constantly getting ahead in matches and then losing his lead. This was even worse in his mind, because he felt his technique was always so much better than his opponents. After watching Mike play a few matches, it became clear that the closer he was to the end of the match the more result-oriented he became and the harder it was for him to focus. We came up with a solution that worked well for Mike. Mike LOVED practicing and was a focused practice player. I told Mike to imagine that in those matches where he got up in the score and was close to winning the match that he was doing a drill. I told him that, just like in practice when he drilled, he needed to have a goal. His goal was to use his serve to set up the point, so he could use his biggest weapon, his forehand. Imagining the point was a drill allowed Mike to focus on the next point and evaluate himself based on whether he stuck to his goal. For Mike, this was an easy transition because he knew how to focus in practice but didn't realize he could do it in matches. Mike is now an incredible competitor and rarely loses matches when he is in the lead.

But what happens if you do not have the support of a good mental tennis coach?

Sports psychologists are typically available in most areas and may be good to add to your support team. They could be a resource you consult with from time to time, but you will want their input on how to implement some positive mental changes in your game. One key piece of advice when consulting with sports psychologists: they like to talk. Often, sports psychologists are just that, psychologists or academics, and their expertise revolves around information. Remember, you do not need information, you need transformation. Your sports psychologist will be tempted to give you tons of information without a definitive plan of action. We want to do one thing at a time, first things first. Have the psychologist give a few suggestions for things that may help, and you will need to decide where you want to implement a change. Then go to the psychologist and be firm with them. Tell them you want to work on X and tell them that you would like their help coming up with a plan to implement just that one area. DO NOT LET THEM ADD MORE STUFF! Make sure they understand that you have a ton of areas to improve and that you can only include one mental piece at a time. If all goes well, you will be back for more help ASAP.

One final option is for you have a main tennis coach for technique and tactics but another coach that you consult with for mental issues. A lot of tennis coaches are not OK with this, so make sure you ask your coach before doing this. Many coaches feel defensive when having to share a player.

Understand that we are all sensitive, fragile human beings parading as confident individuals. Also, most tennis coaches have the same issue as the sports psychologist because they tend to identify too many areas for improvement. If your coach is OK with you going to another coach, the other coach must understand their role. Let them know that you need their help for your mental game and nothing else. Keep your coaches on track. Don't let them take too many tangents in your lessons. That can make things confusing and slow down your progress. Remember that YOU are the client, and they are the service provider, and if you need to be firm about it then do it, your future is worth it!

CHAPTER 8

EMOTIONAL CONTROL

Let's set the stage:

Wimbledon, the hallowed grounds as they say. Two of my favorite tennis players were going at it: Andy Roddick and Roger Federer. In their careers, Roddick had not played Federer at a time when Federer could be beaten. Sure, Roddick technically had a win over him, but Federer might as well have been unbeatable. But this match felt different. Nadal was barreling down on Federer. Each time Federer lost another major, every reporter asked him when he was going to retire. For the first time, Roddick felt like he deserved to be there and had a chance to win. This must have been one of the most difficult tests in Federer's career.

Roddick was serving lights out. Federer could not get a single break of serve for 4 sets. Roddick, up 2 sets to 1, sent the 4th set into a tie-break. Yet at no point did Federer show any signs that he was going to yield. Even though Federer did not show his emotions and continued to compete, Roddick still believed and continued to march closer and closer to what he hoped would be a monumental win over Federer.

Then it happened: Roddick blinked. Roddick missed a crucial high backhand volley put-away in the 4th set tie-break, losing the set. With the match at 2 sets each, you would think that Roddick would go away, and Federer would win it easy... but no. This was a battle all the way to the end. For three and a half hours, both players masterfully served and kept their emotions in check. Roddick, for all his credit, was in complete control emotionally. Roddick showed his emotions more than Federer, but he never let them affect his decision-making or mental state.

At the end of the match, when everything was said and done, Roddick had won more points and more games than Federer, yet Federer held the trophy. With Federer's critics thinking he would never win another major, with Nadal inching closer to Federer's all-time grand slam haul, and with Roddick playing fantastic tennis, Federer kept his cool and never brought his emotions into the game.

So how, with these obstacles happening all at once for Federer, could he maintain control of his emotions? Federer is a great example of emotional control and rightly so. There is a metaphor that perfectly describes Federer's demeanor and accurately shows what good emotional control is:

Your brain can think in three different ways: positively, negatively, and neutrally. Positive and negative are subjective, based on your interpretation of events, while your ability to stay neutral can only happen when you look at things objectively. In that way you are playing a tennis match within the tennis match. On one end of the court is you, but also on your own side is you, and then there is the chair umpire. You on the far end hits a shot that sails a little bit going out. The version of you on the far end interprets the shot as "bad" and is angry. The version of you on the near end wins the point which is "good" and is elated. The you in the umpire chair just says, "Out." The chair umpire is not attached to the outcome, and therefore can judge the situation logically and without emotion.

Be like the chair umpire and look at your mistakes objectively. They are not good or bad but just information that you can use to help you make the next shot.

Remember the idea of being process-oriented versus result-oriented? Federer is the epitome of being process-oriented. He doesn't care that Roddick is playing well, or that his critics will lambast him if he loses yet one more chance at a major. Federer cares about hitting the one shot that he is currently hitting the best way he can. Instead of throwing a hissy fit when he misses, he looks at it objectively. I imagine he thinks, "I hit that ball a little too high, or a little too flat," or, "I shouldn't have hit down the line in that situation." While everyone else is focusing on his results, Federer is too focused on the process to allow his emotions to affect him. Concentrating on the process is the easiest way to gain emotional control.

Being process-oriented becomes a distraction from negative emotions

This starts with good goal setting. When we have something to focus on, we will be distracted from the results. Our goals for ourselves should not be result-oriented goals. Saying, "I want to be number one," or "I want to win today," are not the right kinds of goals. Instead, we should pick goals that focus on the actions that create winning scenarios. The goal would then depend on what we are working on: "I want to make sure my footwork is correct," or, "I will need to focus on my tactics for this match." Process-oriented goals such as those will help us redirect our attention from the emotions that will inevitably crop up. If I miss a shot, I can tell myself that it is OK, that my footwork or tactics were good, and that I just need to keep doing what I am doing, and I will be fine.

128

In between point rituals

Another time when emotions can creep into the match is in between points. During the changeover or directly after a lost point we have more time and sometimes we use that time to dwell on our mistakes or react to our mistakes. This is where between point rituals can help us stay process-oriented instead. We have four things we need to do after playing a point:

- STEP 1- Recover from the previous point
- STEP 2- Use a towel to wipe off your arms, hands, and head
- STEP 3- Strategize what to do with the next point (at least the first two shots)
- STEP 4- Relax your hands and mind before you hit your serve, or if you're returning, be ready to react quickly.

Our in between point rituals distract us from the past as well as the future so that we can focus on the present (which is where optimal performance lies).

When a point is over, we do not have time to throw a tantrum, scream and yell, or do a choreographed dance to show your elation in hitting a good shot. You have a split second to show some emotion, but then you should move on to those four tasks. When those rituals become a priority in our process, we will be nice and distracted from our own emotions because we will have more important things to do. With only 20 seconds in between points and these four important steps to go through, we have very little time for emotions to become a distraction.

How emotional intelligence can help us gain emotional control

When people talk about intelligence, they are normally referring to what is measured in an IQ test: quantitative and verbal reasoning. But those are not the only two forms of intelligence. You as a tennis player show kinesthetic intelligence (body smarts) in the way you have learned how to manipulate your body to strike the ball. There is another important intelligence that can help tennis players that is often overlooked called emotional intelligence. People who are emotionally smart understand their own emotions very well and can also understand their opponent. Both have distinct advantages.

In talking about emotional intelligence, most believe that the way people are born is the way they will always be. "I was born angry. It's in my genes and I can't change it," is a typical mental belief. The reality is that just like your forehand, you can change and improve your temperament as well as any other aspect of your emotional intelligence. Typically, emotional intelligence encompasses self-awareness, self-regulation, social skills, motivation, and empathy. Using the model we used for practice in the first section, how can you come up with a plan for tackling these different areas? As before, pick one area to work on that you and your coach believe would increase your performance. Then you need a way to address the issue. It will take lots of repetition, just like a forehand or backhand. Finally, test your new skill to see how it holds up under pressure.

The area that we most often will focus on is self-regulation. Self-regulation is being able to respond to stimulus in a way that is acceptable, not only spontaneously, but also delaying our emotional response when needed. Self-regulation can take the form of calming ourselves down when we are nervous or stressed, psyching ourselves up when we are low energy or scared, as well as holding off anger when we feel it rising. Remember, in between points you have things to do to be prepared for the next point, and often players waste that time with strong emotional responses that really should be quelled. Even a super strong positive response can have negative repercussions, but the more common way this expresses itself is through anger.

Anger is a terrible emotion for tennis players because tennis relies so deeply on good decision-making. You have thousands of intricate decisions to make in the course of a point (some of which you may not be consciously aware) that need to happen perfectly for you to be successful. In 98% of people, when hooked up to brain scanners and provoked to anger, the part of the brain that is responsible for good decision making is turned off. Even though there is a remaining 2% who can be angry and still make good decisions, the chances of that being you are slim. If you are part of the 2% it's still a dumb idea! Those long emotional tirades zap your energy. One of the in between point necessities is to recover so you can play the next point well. If instead you get angry that becomes much harder to do.

How to stay in your optimal arousal zone

Let's say that you do get angry or overly aroused. This is inevitable if you play enough competitive matches and experience unpredictable situations that arise during competitive play. You will need to know how to calm down. In the heat of the moment that can be challenging, so it is important to have strategies for this.

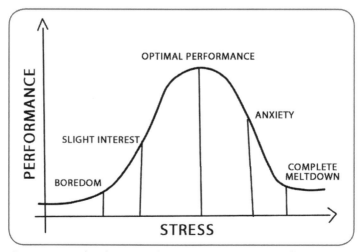

Getting too high or too low can cause issues for players and their performance.

One strategy for calming yourself is to use breathing techniques. It may seem corny but the adage to take a deep breath is scientifically proven to calm you. When you take a deep chesty breath, your lungs press on the small of your back, which activates the vagus nerve that tells your parasympathetic nervous system to chill the F-out. Not only that but focusing on your breathing (something that is happening in the present) is one more way to keep yourself focused. You will not be thinking about what happened in the last point (the past) or that you may not end up winning the match (the future). You have a small window in between the point to get your heart rate and breathing back into an optimal arousal range. If you don't do that you will sacrifice part of your performance and may start to boil over. A strong emotional reaction is not something that happens after one lost point, but it will occur if you let the in between part of your ritual go.

Another easy way to delay a strong emotional response is to do something immediately after a lost point like looking at your strings. Fixing your strings is a good distraction from what just happened and can give your brain a moment to process the mistake before you have an emotional reaction. All it takes is a moment for you to go from a purely emotional state to one where you can make a logical decision.

Anger causes you to make bad decisions, but even after 20 minutes of being calmed down the part of your brain that makes good decisions will STILL be shut off! It is crucial that you delay your emotional response and come up with better, more logical ways to deal with the problem. Allowing yourself to blow up will certainly lead to defeat.

On the opposite end of keeping calm after mistakes is to pump yourself up after a good point. Remember to not get too crazy with your celebration, but often a quick celebratory fist pump is important for getting yourself back into that fighting spirit. If you have not been doing a great job in the match up to that point, it is crucial that you reward yourself when something you do works out for you. Celebrating will help you want to do it again in the future, but it will also show your opponent that you are not giving up and are here to fight. A well-timed fist pump can do wonders for your psyche. The combination of a few fist pumps when you are doing things well with a delayed emotional response when you make mistakes will keep you in an optimal performance zone.

Without going into too much detail, here is a list of things that professional tennis players do to keep themselves feeling relaxed:

1. Rituals: Bouncing the ball or going to the towel helps calm the mind.
2. Music: Listening to music before a match can either pump a player up or calm a player down, depending on the music.
3. Massage: Massage can help a tense muscle during a match and relieve stress before or after.
4. Positive affirmations: Repeating helpful phrases or mantras can help reach an optimal zone.
5. Become social: Talking to a doubles partner can help relieve stress.
6. Laugh it off: Laughing at mistakes instead of giving them too much weight.

7. Perspective: Reminding oneself that it is just one point, that tennis is a game, etc.
8. Mindfulness: Immersing oneself in the surroundings, sights, sounds, and experiences can be a good distraction.

Massage is one way to relax overly tense muscles.

Positive mantras or reminders of what you need to focus on are great ways to relax and stay process oriented.

Talking to your doubles partner can help keep you calm (If you talk to yourself people might think you're weird).

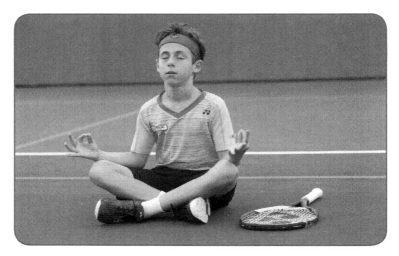

Mindfulness does not require deep introspection like real meditation, just that you accept what you are experiencing and look at your emotions to understand what is happening instead of letting them rule you.

Here are some things professional tennis players do to get themselves pumped up:

1. Talking to themselves: "Come on," or, "keep fighting," or, "you got this" can be helpful. Remember to keep it positive.
2. Fist bumps: A quick fist bump or a clenched fist is great for getting fired up.
3. Intense feet: Physical acts such as bouncing the feet can get arousal levels up.
4. Looking to the crowd: Fans, coaches, or friends watching can help by showing their own passion which helps the player feel the fire.

A strong "come on" or "vamos" can be enough to get you some much needed energy.

It is important that you reward yourself for your successes when you are down in the score as that can pump you up to continue fighting.

An interesting way to look at cheating

The last part of emotional intelligence that we will talk about is empathy. Empathy is understanding the emotions of others and sometimes it can be used to read the emotions of your opponent. You can often feel motivated when your opponent shows obvious signs of frustration or anger. But there are some less obvious cues you can watch for that will give you hope that what you are doing is working.

If you notice your opponent always checks for their coach, parent, or loved ones, this is usually a sign that they are stressed and looking for help. Even if their coach offers them a solution, it probably means they are starting to move out of their optimal stress zone and you are very close to sending them out of their game entirely. Another helpful sign is if your opponent is using gamesmanship or even cheating. You aren't exactly going to miss these things, but you might miss the underlying emotion that caused those actions. You see, if your opponent felt they had to resort to low tactics to beat you, they are probably close to their breaking point. I am not going to cheat if I am confident in winning, am I? Use that knowledge to your benefit instead of letting it upset you (which is what they want).

How self-talk can keep you from becoming negative

When I was first introduced to the idea of positive self-talk, I thought it was stupid. "You're doing great, Jason ole' buddy, just try not to keep missing!" It never felt like it would help me. I don't teach my players this kind of self-talk. It would be hard for me to promote a psychology concept as being helpful if it never did anything for me. I don't think you have to be overly positive in the way you express yourself. In fact, there is a lot of good that can come from simply acknowledging your current emotional state and working within those confines. There are still certain limiting beliefs that hold you back that you can change into self-talk that will promote you to play better. This is what I mean by positive self-talk and not just sending the love of the universe into your racquet.

This is all about manipulating what you are saying from something that hurts you into something that helps you.

> Instead of, "I hate playing a pusher," say, "This will be a challenging opponent for me; I have to concentrate."

That tiny change in the way you phrased things in your head can completely change the way you respond. Typically, as athletes we respond to challenge statements very well. Try to challenge yourself instead of looking at it as a negative.

> Instead of, "I am playing the one seed; there's no way I can win," say, "I want the best opponent because there is more glory in taking out the best. I will have to play well, but that's why I train hard."

This one is weird, and I preface it with a slant on the definition of competition. One definition of competition is to be better than our opponent. The other way is to say that the opponent provides a challenge with which we can make ourselves better. This is one reason we don't like practicing with players who suck (because they are not challenging enough to make us better). Instead say, "Bring it on! Bring on the best," as that attitude will help us play without fear. We can also say,

"Don't hope for your opponent to double fault; instead, want them to get their first serve in." If they get the first serve in, it's more of a challenge (and if we are wanting it to go in, we will be more alert and ready to pounce, which will give us the best chance of getting it back, which means this thinking is a big win-win as it helps us with our self-talk and our reactions!).

Your opponent provides you with a challenge that you get to jump over. They are not your enemy but are in fact necessary for your improvement.

Another important part of self-talk is understanding what your inner voice is actually saying. When we learn to analyze our thoughts, we can gain a deeper understanding of the problems we are having and face them from a logical place.

When I say, "I hate playing pushers," what I am really saying is I do not have a consistent weapon. I can come to that conclusion if I look more deeply at the problem.

First, I would say to myself, "Why do I hate pushers?"

Then I would say, "Well, it is because they get so many balls back that I miss before I can finish off the point."

Then I ask myself, "Why can't I finish off the point without making mistakes?"

To which I would conclude, "I don't have a consistent weapon." (That weapon could be a good forehand to hit winners with or being able to close off the point at the net after a good attack ball.)

Use this process to identify the issue and deal with it before it disrupts your ability to perform.

For instance, "I have to win, or my parents will hate me," might mean that your parents are putting unnecessary pressure on you and you need to talk to them about it, or it might mean that you incorrectly attribute your self-worth with the outcome of the match. Instead say, "If I fight hard, my parents will be proud and so will I. I need to focus." You need to have a way to lose in which you are happy with yourself, and usually that comes from having good process-oriented goals.

Or, "My whole country is counting on me to win this," might mean that you are feeling nervous or it could be true if you are in a Davis or Fed Cup match. Either way, you need a distraction from that pressure. Combine your love for country with a challenge statement and that might do the trick. Try saying, "I have a great opportunity to show my country how hard I can fight. Win or lose, I will concentrate on my footwork so that they can see how hard I fight!"

Story time

I helped a player named Tati (not her real name) with her self-talk. She feels a lot of pressure from her parents and fans because she is one of the best young players in her country. This pressure was starting to creep into the way she talked to herself and it was having a negative impact on her ability to perform. We worked on setting up good process-oriented goals that she could use as the challenge. As her mindset shifted to being process-oriented, she was able to better handle the distractions and outside pressure. Win or lose, Tati could tell herself things like, "My effort is visible, and that is what my country and parents want to see. If I can use my best footwork and use all my effort, I give myself the best chance of winning. That is the best I can do!" Not only is this a healthier way to approach competition, but it helped her win one of her first ever professional matches at the young age of 17. With the right self-talk, we set ourselves up for that type of success.

CHAPTER 9

FOCUS/CONCENTRATION

I hate the word focus. Go to a tennis court anywhere and you will hear this word thrown around, but it seldom is used correctly. Nine out of ten times, if you hear someone say focus, either as a coach to their player, or a player to themselves, what they are saying is, "You missed you *IDIOT*, **focus** on *making* the next shot." If you haven't already guessed, this is highly *result*-oriented. Just telling yourself to focus or yelling at a student to focus will do absolutely nothing without some context and the right confines.

Nideffer's Theory

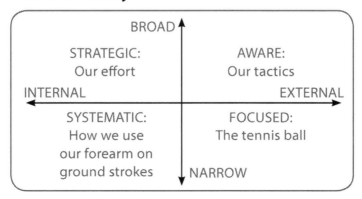

Knowing where to focus and at what time is a huge deal during a tennis point.

Notice that focus is more complicated than most realize. At any given time on the court, your focus may need to shift from being internal/broad to external/broad (aware), then external/narrow (focused) to internal/narrow (systematic).

"How can that be? Isn't focusing just doing my best?" you might be asking yourself.

If you are hitting a forehand your thinking may be on using your whole body, which would be internal (your body) and broad (the whole damn body, and not just your arm or feet).

Then as the ball leaves you may need to shift to external (the court) and broad ("Where the heck are the ball and my opponent?").

As your opponent hits the ball, your attention may shift again to external (once again something outside of you since you are not your opponent) and narrow (the ball).

Finally, as you hit it again, this time as a volley, you might be working on your backswing and will be thinking about not taking your arm behind your body which is internal (inside your body) but narrow (your arm compared to your whole body).

On the changeover you may want to analyze your stroke which would be internal, or you may want to analyze your strategy which is external.

In between points you will sometimes focus on your breathing which is internal, and then before you serve you will be thinking about your target which is external.

With all this shifting attention, to truly **focus** means...

...to be thinking about the *right* thing, at the right **time.**

Instead of yelling at yourself to focus, it is better to remind yourself of where your focus *should* have been. This is based on what you are working on and what was happening at that moment. *Where* your focus is will depend on a myriad of factors outlined below because, as you now know, focus can be multi-directional.

Pre-competition vs. competition focus

If you remember the first section of the book, you learned how your training schedule and proper periodization could help you better retain your skills. One part of this is the difference between where your thoughts need to be when you are in pre-competition mode versus competition mode.

Typically, during a training block you will be learning new things that require a lot of internal focus. As you enter pre-competition mode, you will have worked them to a point where they do not require as much conscious thought. However, you still need to focus on these things to keep implementing them under pressure. That is why you should do lots and lots of repetitions in a controlled environment and then also give yourself some practice sets and situations where you can continue to focus on these changes. It is important to not give yourself too much to focus on, as it can be overwhelming.

As you get closer to the competition phase, the more well-rehearsed these skills should be, and they should eventually slip into your unconscious. That will allow for some of your focus to shift back to other important areas, but this won't happen overnight. You cannot afford to just flip a switch when you play sets or practice matches and say, "If I didn't learn it yet I won't ever learn it."

Sometimes focusing on your changes will negatively impact your performance (in the short term). But it is still important for you to have some matches where the focus is on the changes (remember that these can be technical or tactical, physical or mental, so learn to isolate the area you are working on in your focus). The hope is that if you give it enough time and energy, by the time you transition to the competition phase you will have done it enough that you will not be *distracted* by your changes.

Disclaimer: YES! Thinking about your changes is a distraction that will hurt your performance in the short-term. This is a big problem for many tennis players because it makes them fearful of the necessary changes that will ultimately help them improve. If you learn to focus your attention on the right thing at the right time, you can maximize your training while also maximizing your results.

Story time:

As a child I remember always being beaten by a local player named Brian. Brian had started his tennis journey earlier than me and had been a nationally ranked junior. The problem was that Brian was, for lack of a better word, a "pusher." Brian won this way as a young player. Because he was winning, he had little incentive to develop his weapons, learn how to volley, or change anything about his technique (even if it was obviously needed).

Because why change something that wins, am I right?

This mentality came back to haunt Brian when as seventeen-year-olds I was finally able to beat him in an important sectional tournament and our two paths started to diverge. Brian never developed beyond that earliest version of himself while I continued to improve. This is not an isolated story, as I see this exact problem all the time. I was willing to put in some *"suck time"* while I **developed** those skills, even signing up for tournaments with the intention of *working* on things instead of settling for the status quo.

The zone

Now it's competition time. Best case scenario, you have honed your skills, you have effectively integrated your changes into your regimen, and you are a lean mean fighting machine.

Where should your focus now be?

I have heard coach after coach say things like, "Don't think. Thinking is what keeps you out of the zone.

There is a lot of talk in the sporting world about "the zone."

I say **screw** the zone, and here's why...

Let me tell you about the zone:

"Everything is flowing."

"You can do no wrong, you are perfectly in the moment, and the ball is the size of a watermelon."

Sounds amazing, right? Well, guess what?

You will never be in the zone.

You know what is funny about the zone?

Just being aware that you are in the zone will distract you enough to bring you out of the zone.

Try too hard to get into the zone?

That's a perfect way to never get there.

If you think that everything needs to be in *perfect* harmony with birds sing-songing in your ear as you hit every ball to win, then you are sunk. Learn how to focus, and then re-focus when you lose focus, and the zone becomes a happy accident that will roll around once in every blue moon. Learn to depend on yourself, and don't expect that you will play well because the reality of competition is that you will need to learn to win *without your best* to obtain consistent results.

Tennis is hard and there is nothing you can do to magically make hitting the tennis ball on the sweet spot easier.

Focusing during competition can be difficult. Given what you know about Nideffer's Theory of Attentional Focus, with so much going on, how do you focus? Focusing on your changes can be a distraction. If you have not rehearsed correctly and your changes are not well-ingrained, then you have a difficult choice to make.

On the one hand, if you focus on your changes, you will not play at your best. On the other, if you do *not* focus on your changes, you will need to go back to learning those important areas that you worked on during training. You will have slowed your progress.

Remember, these changes were well thought out and picked for their ability to improve performance in the long-term. Essentially, by NOT focusing on your changes you doom yourself in the long-term for the tradeoff of short-term success.

The tennis coach in me says go with the long-term goal and focus on your changes. The human in me says, "It depends." If Wimbledon is on the line, screw your changes. Most of the time there will not be that much weight on the tournaments you play, and it is OK if you do not perform at 100%. Besides, as we already discussed, good luck at ever achieving 100% performance. You might as well stick to your changes, and then find a way with what you have to win.

> The magic we can conjure in just 20 seconds, or the spell we can put ourselves under. How our in between point rituals can help us focus.

With all this stuff to focus on, do you think that you can focus if you are emotionally charged?

Probably not, in fact, statistically speaking, FOR SURE not.

What was one of the things we did to help control our emotions?

That's right, our in between point rituals.

When thinking about the between point rituals, I am often reminded of a special moment from my childhood that I want to share with you to help you understand their importance.

It was 2005, before Tiger Woods was marred by scandals and knee surgeries that held him back. He was at his best and on his way to the top of the golf world. In the Masters Tournament (like a tennis grand-slam tournament), Tiger went into a thrilling playoff with another player and ended up winning in a sudden death playoff hole. What a lot of people forget is that he nearly lost it on the 16th hole. Tiger had a dreadful drive and was left with a 20-foot chip to keep himself afloat. This was the golf equivalent of needing to hit a tweener lob winner on the dead sprint after tracking down a drop shot. Tiger made this shot, but what stood out to me as a young athlete was what he said in the post-tournament conference. A reporter stood up and asked him, "Tiger, with so much on the line, all your fans watching, money, fame, the works, what were you thinking about?"

Tiger started describing how he stands over a golf ball and gets ready to hit it. It was something like, "I was think-ing about how when I use my chip, I take a pretty short backswing, and I was thinking about breathing, and I was thinking about all this other boring golf stuff..."

The reporter asked, "Come on, why weren't you thinking about how important the shot was, and how you had a big lead and might have blown it?"

Tiger calmly said, "If I was thinking about all that stuff how could I have possibly made the shot?"

Just like Tiger Woods in golf, our in between point rituals can help us focus just like Tiger's rituals before hitting his chip.

We talked a lot about how important our in between point rituals are for calming our emotions and helping us prevent an emotional uprising. Another important benefit of between point rituals is to help us *stay focused*.

It is common to get distracted by the gravitas of the moment or the seriousness of the next point. Well guess what? YOU CAN'T CONTROL WHO WINS AND WHO LOSES THAT NEXT POINT! Thinking about it only causes you to focus on the wrong thing.

Fixing our strings gives our brains something to do besides dwell on past mistakes. It is in the present and the present is where focused attention typically occurs.

One of the most important things you can remind yourself of is that distractions are not real. YES! That's right! A distraction is just you *focusing* on the **wrong** thing at that moment. In between the points you should be *focused* on our rituals. All too often players let their eyes wander and the distractions mount.

This is when staying process-oriented becomes so important. So many things can shift your focus, and it is important to have a strong routine for between the points. The first step is to have something to do immediately to prevent you from reacting to emotions. Give your brain a moment to think logically. Have a celebratory fist pump or "vamos" for when you do something well or quickly turn around and look at your strings if you mess up.

That keeps your focus in the present and on your rituals instead of the whole host of devils that want to sway your attention elsewhere.

You still have time for your thoughts to stray to things that get you in trouble. You might start double-guessing your strategy or get down on yourself or think about the weight of the moment.

Instead, you need to **distract** yourself in a *good* way by thinking about all that boring tennis stuff, just like Tiger thought about all his boring golf stuff. Go to the towel and take some deep breaths. Then, walk up to the line. Think about where you want to hit the first two shots if all goes according to plan.

More deep breaths.

Relax your hand and think about how to execute a good serve.

It seems so easy, yet to reach the point where you only think about this and not everything else is basically impossible. Those extra thoughts will find ways to penetrate your thinking. All you can do is continuously remind yourself to think the proper thoughts...

... If that seems too hard, remember, how can you possibly play a good point otherwise?

Tiger Woods understands this. Tiger Woods immerses himself in the mundane details of preparing to hit his putt and then how to hit the putt. If you want to play highly focused points, start with strong rituals that can keep you focused on the process-oriented aspects of competition.

The *Most* Important Place to Focus!

I have beaten around the bush long enough. I'm finally ready to talk about what we *should* focus on during a match. Before I tell you, I need to explain a little more about your brain.

There is a difference between an awareness and a conscious thought. You are aware of thousands of things at once. You are aware of the weight of your shirt on your shoulders, but you weren't consciously thinking about it until I mentioned it to you. (Did I just blow your mind? That happened to me when someone pulled this trick on me.) While some studies seem to believe we can, at times, in certain scenarios, contain up to four conscious thoughts at once, for all intents and purposes, let's say we can only have one. While we do shift our focus from one place to another (as we discussed with Nideffer's Theory), we can't focus on all those things at the same time. If you are thinking about your tactics when you should be thinking about your swing, you will mess up your swing. If you are thinking about your swing when you should be thinking about your feet, you will mess up your footwork.

Breaking that down one step further, for an athletic action to be correct, the thought that we are currently having will have to match the action that we are trying to have. Focusing is very complex because it requires a timing element that creates complex scenarios like, "If I am working on X, I need to think about X, even if I should be thinking about Y," and, "I was focusing on Z. Even though I was technically focused, at that moment it would have been better to have been thinking about W." This is SUPER interesting in the context of all sports, not just tennis. Let me give you an example:

I was watching the Super Bowl between the Ravens and the Giants when I was in high school. This was back when the Ravens relied on field goals and defensive touchdowns to win games. The Ravens had a beast of a defense led by Ray Lewis, and a "please just don't screw this up for us" offense. Ray Lewis was such a presence that he must have been very distracting for the other team. Multiple times the Giants quarterback threw interceptions, and multiple times the ball was put in a catchable place, only for the receiver to drop the ball. How does a professional athlete drop a catchable ball? You can often tell by looking at their eyes. Right as they were about to make the catch, you could see their eyes shift, almost as if to say, "Holy crap, I hope I don't get destroyed by Ray Lewis right after catching this ball." Ray Lewis was so intimidating that players would be forced to think either, "brace for impact," or, "I need to make a cut, so I don't get hit."

What this ultimately does is shift their attention away from the thought they should be having, which is, "Catch the dang ball." Since you cannot have a "brace for impact" thought and perform a "catch the ball" action at the same time, they would screw up. Long live Ray Lewis and Ravens football!

In the above scenario, the timing is super important. Had the player focused *first* on catching the ball, and *then* bracing for impact, he would have been able to catch the ball AND brace for impact. The fear involved in the situation caused a lapse in focus. In tennis players, this presents itself most often when you are hitting the ball. You cannot have a "Hit the ball" action, with a "Where's my shot going?" thought. Sequentially, the timing is important. You must first hit the ball the best you can, and then, and only then, can you shift your focus to where your shots are going.

Catching a football is easy, but try catching it when someone is about to tackle you and see how difficult it becomes. My son Blake was not harmed in the making of this photo.

Becoming overly concerned with winning or losing will have negative effects on your ability to focus. The moment you care more about whether your shot goes in, as opposed to hitting the ball well, is the moment you lose focus and miss or hit a lower quality shot. This does not mean that you should be *unaware* of whether your shots go in or not. Tactically, if you are missing too much, you will need to make some adjustments. You may need to aim for larger targets or hit safer shots, and that is OK. But what remains paramount is we need to hit the ball well FIRST AND FOREMOST, regardless of whether it is working out for us or not.

The Hitting Eye

I alluded to the player's eyes in the football example. Your eyes are super cool, and I'd like to share some facts about your eyes to help me explain my next point. It has been said that the eyes are a gateway to the soul. Believe it or not, your eyes will follow your primary thought which could give someone watching your eyes insight into your soul (or at least what might be on your mind). In fact, every time your thought changes, your eyes shift.

Have you ever heard of R.E.M. sleep? R.E.M. stands for rapid eye movement and means that your eyes shift every time your thoughts shift, amped up to eleven. When you go into R.E.M. sleep, your eyes move back and forth in your skull up to 1000 times per minute. It's no wonder that R.E.M. sleep is often when we dream. Have you ever had a dream that felt like it lasted a long time, but the reality is it was only ten minutes of actual time? With all those thoughts happening so quickly it can feel like more time has elapsed.

As a spectator, you can see when a player has this problem. Right as they are about to hit the ball, you see their eyes shift. It is not just as simple as saying, "Keep your head still," which might have technical and balance value, but *does not* aid concentration. Controlling your eyes will control your focus.

How the heck do I do that?

To hit a tennis ball well, you must have the hitting thought (the thought must match the action). For your eyes to be focused on the hit, they will need to be looking at your anticipated contact point.

Why anticipated contact and not actual contact?

Can you *see* contact?

Sadly, no.

Past 30 mph your eyes lag behind the ball, so you will not see anything (if you do, it is your mind creating an image for memories sake, not a real image), but by watching where you think contact will be, you will focus on hitting the ball and not be distracted by where the ball ends up going.

How long do you need to keep your eyes still and watch the anticipated contact point?

Only for as long as you are hitting.

Once you are finished hitting, you can now have a new thought, which would be a combination of, "Where did my ball go?" or "Did it do damage?" or "What can my opponent do here?" or "Where should I position myself?"

The important thing to remember is that hitting the ball extends all the way until you finish. As an advanced player, you likely swing fast, which means you only need to keep your eyes still at contact for a quarter of a second or so *past* when you hit the ball. While this may feel like an eternity to you, you have plenty of time to do this and still be ready for the next shot.

Here you can see the player's eyes focused on watching anticipated contact.

Here you can see the player has kept their head still, but has shifted their eyes to look across the net.

Here you can see the player is not only looking across the net but has also pulled his head up with his eyes, which would have negative consequences for focus as well as technique.

The Best at Watching Anticipated Contact

If you have been paying attention to tennis for the past 17 years, you have seen someone perform this concentration task perfectly, Roger Federer. There are others who have done this masterfully. If you prefer a female role model, Billie Jean King comes to mind. Study their eyes and emulate this trait and you will be well on your way to performance mastery and **real** focus that will help you hit the ball to the best of your ability.

Mind tricks

One thing I do to help me focus is to trick myself into it. As you have seen, it is easy to get distracted in tennis and lose focus because of the score. No matter how good you become at tennis concentration, you will never stop wanting to win. You will always be susceptible to the score being a distraction. You can trick yourself out of this result-oriented focus with special self-talk aimed at the problem. You likely do not find it difficult to concentrate during drills since there is no pressure. What I do to help me achieve that kind of focus during a match is to say to myself that my opponent is now my coach or ball feeder. I imagine that they are just testing me. This isn't a point in a match, but a drill. Sure, it is a drill where I have no idea where the ball is going, but it's a drill nonetheless. In this drill, I am evaluated by how well I make decisions and how well I can concentrate. If I make good decisions and concentrate on my execution, I will most likely win. If I don't, at the very least I know that I gave this match my best concentrated effort and I did not let the score get in the way of my decision-making or focus.

Now, no matter how good I am at concentrating, if this match ends up close, there will be some important points that will test my ability to tune out the score. When those important moments come up, I have one more Jedi mind trick at my disposal. This is where my knowledge of how mental focus works will help me. I tell myself that no matter how good my opponent is, I have been practicing correct mental focus for much longer than they have, and I have been doing it correctly. Unless they have read this book, they probably aren't as strong mentally as I am. Knowing that I will not be the first player to 'blink" gives me the confidence I need to put forth my best focused effort for that important point. Of course, it is possible that I will lose the point anyway, but I can't afford to think that in the moment. All I can do is focus to the best of my ability and allow the chips to fall as they may. Without a doubt, I will win more points giving my best focused effort instead of allowing my mental game to be distracted by the score or anything else.

CONCLUSION

One year ago, I decided to write this book. This is my beginning to end, everything you will ever need, all the resources to succeed system of training for you to become a professional tennis player. Yet I left out one important part. No matter how well you train or how well put together you are as a player, there will always be an unforeseen and unexpected flip-of-the-coin nature to competing one-on-one. This might be your opponent playing out of their mind that day, or an unlucky net-chord. For this book, I shared the structure for developing a player, but a developmental structure does not have a final chapter.

As a player, you can never stop. You will continue to look for ways to improve because everyone around you will be doing the same and *they* won't stop. When you are writing a book there is an end. Perhaps tennis has an end too, since at some point we all must retire from attempting professional success. For me that retirement was when my first son was born. For some it is a career-ending injury. Hopefully for you it will be at the end of many years of successful professional tennis, thanks to you having learned a good pathway from this book.

The sad reality is that most of your peers will not make a living at playing this sport. No matter how well you follow my system, you have zero guarantee that any system will work. Tennis is not an *if X then Y* situation, but more of an *if X then there is a chance of Y* scenario.

Here's the good news: I want you to succeed. Want more good news? I don't want to leave you hanging. Because you purchased this book, you put a tremendous amount of faith in me and my system. I am going to help as best as I can. You are cordially invited to be a part of my community where I will be there for you whenever you need a little help or encouragement. Of course, it is not possible for me to help every one of you in person, but I will be as much of a resource for you as I possibly can be. There is a secret Facebook group that you are invited to join if you send proof of purchase of this book to the following e-mail: Jason@tenniscircuitry.com. When you access the Facebook group, you can post your questions and I will personally answer them. Not only that, everyone who bought the book will be an extended resource for you. They will be players and coaches who have been through what you have and will be able to offer their help as well. We will become a hive mind, stronger together than we could ever be apart.

Thank you for your purchase and I wish you the best of luck on your journey to the top!

ACKNOWLEDGEMENTS

I would like to thank my beautiful wife for encouraging me in all of my endeavors. I would like to thank my two sons Blake and Alex for being a constant source of joy (and also frustration). I would like to thank my editor Lisa for being an incredible help in getting my cruddy English into something you could all understand. I would like to thank my students for listening to me even when I am clearly full of it. I would like to thank my parents for giving me the opportunity to pursue my passions in life. And finally, I would like to thank my many influences but namely my coaches at the Tennis Institute in Baltimore, Maryland, for being such an important part of my formative years. Lenny, Thiha, Matt and Kristen are some of the best coaches in the world and I wouldn't be half the player or person that I am today without them.

ABOUT THE AUTHOR

Jason Goldman-Petri is the author of the series "Tennis Circuitry" and the go-to Video Analysis Expert and Tennis Strategy Speaker at IMG Academy. Jason began teaching tennis at the ripe age of 17 and went on to become one of the youngest Tennis Directors of 2 Country Clubs, as well as a Head Tennis Pro at IMG Academy all before the age of 30. ACE Certified and a Certified Tennis Performance Specialist with iTPA, Jason is one of only 1000 USTA High Performance Certified Coaches and one of only 50 Tennis Coaches in the world selected for the USPTR Master of Tennis in Performance Certification.

While studying at the prestigious Johns Hopkins University, where he graduated in 2008 with a Bachelor of Arts in Psychology, Jason Goldman-Petri got his start as a Tennis Coach working at the Bare Hills Racquet and Fitness Club as a part of The Tennis Institute. There, he was personally trained and Certified by his long-time mentor Lenny Scheuerman, who coached several world-ranked players, including former Wimbledon doubles champion JoAnn Russell. Jason also served as the Assistant Men's and Women's Tennis Coach at Stevenson University for three years. Later, he was promoted to the Head Men's And Women's Tennis Coach. During this time, Jason served as an Assistant Coach at Roland Park Country School where he helped lead the Varsity team to four-straight MIAA Conference championships from 2008-2011. He also served as the Head JV Coach and Head Middle School Coach at Notre Dame Prep. Having coached extensively at various levels, Jason has trained players to transition from the Juniors directly to playing professionally, from the Juniors to top level college tennis teams, and from college tennis to the pro tour.

As a player, Jason was a member of the men's team from Wilmington, Delaware that captured the national title at the 2011 USTA League 4.5 Adult National Championships held at the Jim Reffkin Tennis Center in Tucson, Arizona. He was also a member of the Green Spring Racquet Club's Men's USTA Tri-Level Yellow Team that won the Mid-Atlantic Sectional championship on Jan. 23, 2011. Jason was ranked in the top 150 of the Mid-Atlantic USTA Open rankings and in the top 50 players in Maryland through the Men's Open Ranking. He was the runner-up in 2010 for the Maryland State Men's Indoor Championship and finished 12th in the Men's Open Singles of the final 2009 Maryland Adult/Senior Rankings.

Today, Jason Goldman-Petri is a World-Class Tennis Coach with a talent for coaching players to go Pro. If you're ready to make the transition to becoming a Professional Tennis Player, Jason is the coach for you.